God calls us to b

ONE

SIMPLE ACT OF

OBEDIENCE

FRED J. KROPP

Discover the God - Adventure life you were meant to live!

A wholly owned subsidiary of **TBN**

One Act of Obedience

Trilogy Christian Publishers A Wholly Owned Subsidiary of Trinity Broadcasting Network

2442 Michelle Drive Tustin, CA 92780

Rights Department, 2442 Michelle Drive, Tustin, CA 92780.

Trilogy Christian Publishing/TBN and colophon are trademarks of Trinity Broadcasting Network.

Cover design by: Trilogy

For information about special discounts for bulk purchases, please contact Trilogy Christian Publishing.

Trilogy Disclaimer: The views and content expressed in this book are those of the author and may not necessarily reflect the views and doctrine of Trilogy Christian Publishing or the Trinity Broadcasting Network.

Manufactured in the United States of America

10 9 8 7 6 5 4 3 2 1

Library of Congress Cataloging-in-Publication Data is available.

ISBN: 978-1-68556-609-8

E-ISBN: 978-1-68556-610-4

DEDICATION

I dedicate this book to the Christians who took the time and risk to tell me the good news of Jesus Christ even when I rejected them. I have eternal life today because of them, and I am forever grateful! May the Lord fill us all with the compassion and love that motivated their lives!

ACKNOWLEDGMENTS

Not only will you hear the passion, drive, and love Fred offers, but you will be challenged to press into God's purpose for you. You can go into all your world and proclaim and demonstrate the power of God. Get ready to be changed in a very good way.

—Dr. Gary Howse
P91 Ministries, counselor/teacher

"One Simple Act of Obedience" by Fred Kropp is one of the most powerful, life-changing books I have ever read. How many times in the past have we as believers let fear of rejection keep us from becoming obedient, bold, miracle-working witnesses for Jesus in our daily lives? The last words Jesus spoke to His believers before He ascended back to heaven are found in Acts 1:8, "But you shall receive power when the Holy Spirit has come upon you; and you shall be witnesses to Me in Jerusalem, and in all Judea and Samaria, and to the end of the earth." Since these are the last words Jesus spoke, they are the ones He wanted His believers to remember and obey above all else. Reading "One Simple Act of Obedience" is a real life-changer! Fear of being rejected when it comes to being a bold, "miracle-working witness" for Jesus will become a thing of the past. You will want to tell others about this powerful book and buy copies for many of your Christian friends.

—Dr. A. L. Gill
Founder of Gill Ministries International Outreach

We have at our disposal a lethal weapon that is able to disarm powers of darkness and to change the hardest heart in one moment. What is that? It is the Good News of the Kingdom of God through our Lord, Jesus Christ. But how do we set off this ticking time bomb? How do we deliver this amazing package? My comrade and friend of years, Fred Kropp, says it best, "One Simple Act of Obedience." One morning the voice of the Holy Spirit came to me saying, "I will have a revival of kindness." Isn't that a novel idea? Better yet, wouldn't that be an amazing thing to witness, let alone be a participant? According to Kropp's book, we should be expecting this and so much more!

—James W. Goll
Founder of God Encounters Ministries GOLL Ideation LLC
Author, communication coach, recording artist, and friend of God

I had the honor of interviewing Pastor Fred one evening for a Facebook Live. He began to speak of Romans 5:19: through one man's obedience, many become righteous. Then, he began to tell story after story of his life when he simply responded to the Lord's voice in doing "One Simple Act of Obedience." These stories were full of miracles, salutations, and healings. He made it seem so easy to actually walk daily in one simple act of obedience. Each chapter and testimony will ignite your own prayer life and your desire to respond to God's personal invitations to step out with one simple act of obedience.

—Julie Meyer
Author of 30 Days of Praying The Psalms, Singing The Scriptures
24/7 Worship Radio, Into the River Online Worship Community
Healing Rooms Apostolic Center in Santa Maria, California

Some communicators speak to the head. Others speak to the heart. A select few have the amazing ability to speak to both. Pastor Fred Kropp is one of these. His new book, "One Simple Act of Obedience," addresses a deep universal need to find genuine purpose in life that can only be found in Jesus. The intimate stories and real-life testimonies throughout not only enable you to relate but ignite a fire inside of you to lay your life in the palm of the Father's hand and live in obedience and faith to the voice of Jesus. You are reminded that even if you don't feel capable or good enough, He (Jesus) has chosen and qualified you to fulfill the calling and destiny He has placed upon your life. I believe that God will use this book to bring restoration, healing, and refreshment to your heart that you didn't even know you needed.

—Justin Jacobs
Lead Pastor of The Bridge Central Coast

This book is a testimony of the faithfulness of God when we choose to walk in faith and obedience to Him. Fred's experiences in this book are designed to encourage and stimulate the next generation of believers to demonstrate the kingdom of God through their lives. There are many insights and nuggets of wisdom that will equip the believer to shine for Jesus in this generation.

—Rick and Lori Taylor
Healing Rooms Apostolic Center Santa Maria, California
US Directors for the Healing Rooms Global Network

I have known Fred Kropp for over fifty years as a good friend, a colleague in ministry, and partner in a number of mission adventures. What he has shared in this book are the real-life experiences of being led by the Holy Spirit and the effects that just one life and one act of obedience can have in the lives of so many. His life has impacted ours, for sure. I am so glad Fred has taken the time to document so many of the supernatural encounters and miracles he has experienced. I know that each one who reads this book will be extremely blessed and encouraged into making your own acts of obedience.

—James Reimer
Missionary church-planter and
founder of Strategic Indigenous Missions

"One Simple Act of Obedience" has something for everyone! It is a book that speaks to kingdom principles that are foundational for both new and mature believers. The words of Jesus Christ are still ringing out, "Beseech the Lord of the Harvest to thrust out workers into the harvest field." Fred heard the command, and this book is the memoir of the exciting and dramatic exploits of a man (and his wife!) who walked accordingly. Young believers, would you like to learn how to walk in obedience and in the Spirit? This book is for you. Mature believers, it is never too late to return to a life of adventure and spiritual vitality in your walk with God. This book will show the way!

—Andy Caldwell
Christian Radio Talk Show host

Pastor Fred Kropp's ability to connect dots in life is inspiring. This book will encourage you to see everything that happens in your past, present, and future through the lens of the Holy Spirit and His providence. This is an encouraging book that you will return to often to get the motivation to look behind the scenes of your circumstance and see the Lord changing earth because heaven has been moved by your prayers. Some call it "50/20 vision," Genesis 50:20, "As for you, you meant evil against me, but God meant it for good in order to bring about this present result, to keep many people alive." Fred's book will give you 50/20 vision.

—Paul Berry
Senior Pastor Calvary Chapel Santa Maria, California

The book you hold in your hand is an invitation into the life of faith-in-action and everyday obedience to which every Christian is called. Through these pages, Pastor Fred will inspire you to live the life you were created for and give you practical application on how to naturally walk in the supernatural. Reading this book will give you more than mere information and inspiration. I believe it will be an impartation!

—Jeff Peterson
Founding Pastor of Authentic
Church in Orange County, California

TABLE OF CONTENTS

INTRODUCTION

Recently I have been arrested by one phrase, "By one man's obedience, many will be made righteous." It is a quote from the Apostle Paul's letter to the church in Rome.

"For as by one man's disobedience many were made sinners, so also by one Man's obedience many will be made righteous" (Romans 5:19).

The "one man" refers to Jesus Christ. His one act of obedience in going to the cross has made all those who believe and trust in Him for forgiveness by His blood righteous before God.

As I meditated on the phrase "One man's obedience, many will be made righteous," I saw it as the key trigger to revival and seeing the power of God move through each one of us. Once I saw this, I began to see that there are all kinds of examples of one act of obedience throughout the Bible.

The goal of this book is to activate Christ in you, the hope of glory, and open your eyes to the power of "one act of obedience." The stories I share and Bible examples I give will excite you, stimulate you, encourage and build your faith to see that your one act of obedience will release God's supernatural power through your life.

For many years the body of Christ has been praying, fasting, and believing God for an outpouring of the Holy Spirit here in America like we see in Acts, chapter 2. I can tell you that our prayers have moved the hand of God, and revival is here now! Now the Lord is looking for ordinary Christians like you and me, who are willing to hear His voice and step out in faith and do "one act of obedience." When we do, we will see the presence and power of God come alive through our lives. We will never be the same again.

What would happen if hundreds of thousands of Jesus followers started doing "one act of obedience"? I'll tell you what will happen! Millions of people will encounter the presence and power of God, and multitudes would come into the kingdom of God and be eternally transformed.

I am basing the core message of this book on three main scriptures:

> *For as by one man's disobedience many were made sinners, so also by one Man's obedience many will be made righteous.*
>
> **Romans 5:19**

> *I beseech you therefore, brethren, by the mercies of God, that you present your bodies a living sacrifice, holy, acceptable to God, which is your reasonable service.*
>
> **Romans 12:1**

> *God has chosen the foolish things of the world to shame the wise, and God has chosen the weak things of the world to shame the things which are strong, and the insignificant*

things of the world and the despised God has chosen, the things that are not, so that He may nullify the things that are, so that no man may boast before God.

1 Corinthians 1:27–29 (NASB)

These three verses have powerfully transformed my life through the years, and they will do the same in your life as well. By the end of this book, you will not only have memorized them, but you will experience the power of these scriptures released in you!

Since I have been preaching and teaching people the Word of God for over forty years, I have learned a few things. One, I don't have the answers to everything. I try to stick with talking about things that I know are true because the Bible says they are. Two, I don't like trying to answer questions that no one is asking. It is a waste of my time and for those who are listening. At the same time, it is good to stimulate one another to love and do good deeds even if it isn't something we want to be challenged by. Three, I like messages that don't just inspire me but give me practical things or tools that I can apply to my life and see results. Four, I want to speak from my own experience of walking with Jesus and applying the truth of His Word in my life so that others may experience what I have learned from my successes and failures.

Who Is This Book Written For?

This book is for those who desire to see Jesus Christ exalted in their life, whether by life or by death, as the

Apostle Paul states in Philippians one, verse twenty. Those who want to be inspired, awakened, challenged, and activated in making an eternal difference in the lives of people around them. Those who want to see the kingdom of God manifested through their lives daily. This book is designed to stimulate and activate the potential of Christ in you, the hope of glory!

In Jesus' prayer in the Gospel of John, chapter 17, Jesus said, "As You (speaking of the Father) sent me into the world, I also have sent them into the world." In other words, we are sent by Jesus to accomplish the same mission He was sent by the Father to accomplish. To seek and save those who are lost. To declare the kingdom of God is at hand and demonstrate it with God's power working through us. To show the world who God the Father truly is and to demonstrate His love, compassion, and generosity to those in need. To make disciples of all ethnicities and nationalities. To glorify and magnify Jesus Christ through our lives. And to live out the adventure He planned for our lives before the foundation of the world. If these things excite you, then this book is for you.

I want to see you run the race that God has set before you and win the eternal prizes He has awaiting you for all eternity. I want you to hear Him say, "Well done, good and faithful servant! You have been faithful in a few things; I will give you authority over many things! Enter into the joy of the Lord!"

Lastly, I want to make it very clear that even though I tell a lot of stories about my own experiences, it is not about me but about what Jesus Christ has done in me and through me. Apart from Jesus, I am nothing and can do nothing outside of His grace, mercy, and love. The more I abide in Him and He in me, the more I see acts of obedience happen in my everyday life. All the glory and praise go to Him and Him alone.

—Pastor Fred Kropp

Chapter One

MY LIFE BEFORE JESUS

In this book, you are going to learn several things about how to live your life from an eternal perspective. Before we go there, allow me to share the first few chapters telling the story of how I came to know that Jesus is God. I was born on May 9, 1948, in San Jose, California. I am part of the post-war baby boomer generation, the oldest of three sons. My father was a construction worker with a serious drinking problem and deep emotional scars from a tragic childhood which included his father's suicide when he was in the eighth grade. My mother was the daughter of Italian immigrants, a devoted Catholic who hauled us off to Sunday mass every week and sent us to Saturday morning catechism to learn the fundamentals of being Catholic. Fundamentals like reciting the Lord's prayer, praying through the rosary, and understanding the difference between venial and mortal sins. Venial sins would send you to purgatory, a holding place between heaven and hell (where if you did enough penance, you earned the right to graduate to heaven). Mortal sins would send you straight to hell if you died before confessing your sins to the priest on Saturday.

My childhood years were filled with opportunities for rejection. I was bigger than most of the other kids, and they liked to make fun of me. On top of this, my father would punish me for the slightest infraction. Sometimes, I really had it coming. There were times when my father took the punishment a little too far. My parents smoked cigarettes, so one time, I took a pack of my dad's cigarettes and went to the shed in our backyard and tried smoking two cigarettes at the same time. After a few inhales, I started to get sick and turn green. Just then, my dad walked in and caught me. He took the rest of the cigarettes in the pack and held me down, stuffing them in my mouth and making me eat them all. It kept me from smoking for a number of years! There were times when I really deserved his punishments, like when I would beat up my younger brother, Harold, or talk back to my mom! His favorite punishment was making me pull weeds in the front yard while all the other kids walked by my house on their way to play. It contributed to my growing rejection problem. To this day, I don't like yard work. Don't get me wrong, I am thankful for my father's discipline; it taught me to respect authority. I have watched the lives of others who had no discipline at all, and I decided that even bad discipline is better than no discipline. Don't think I am condoning child abuse, but the Bible says, "The rod and rebuke give wisdom, but a child left to himself brings shame to his mother" (Proverbs 29:15).

During these years, my father started going on drunken binges, and we wouldn't see him for three to five days at a time. I'll never forget the time my mother, brother, and I came home to find that he had destroyed what seemed to me like everything that was breakable in the house. It scared my mother enough that we moved to one of our relative's houses in a nearby town, and I started going to another school. As I sat in my classes, I felt like all the students were looking at me like something was wrong with me!

As I moved through my junior high years into high school, I was now coming to the conclusion that I was a less than average person, with less than average looks, less than average intelligence, less than average abilities, living in a less than average family. I was convinced that I was doomed to a less-than-average future. I began resenting anyone who was smart, good-looking, or gifted in sports. I envied their ease in achieving success. I remember going to the annual sports banquet and watching everyone else get an award. I was hurt and angry because I knew I would never be one of those people. I didn't get any support or encouragement from my parents. My father was constantly telling me I was stupid or failing in some way. His own self-rejection was being vented on me. He was only doing to me what his father had done to him.

After graduating from high school, I went to a junior college, not having the grades to get into San Jose State

University, where many of my friends went. During this time, my focus turned toward finding a mate. Because of my lack of self-confidence and past rejection, I usually picked girls who had serious problems themselves. My relationships with these girls always ended in disaster. I experienced one major emotional letdown after another. I came to the place where I was convinced that not only did no one love me, but that there was no such thing as real love. I began to project the rejection of myself onto the girls I dated, believing that if they really knew me, they wouldn't like me. I would pick them up for a date, and from the moment they got into the car, I would begin saying, "You don't really like me, do you?" In a short time, I would convince them, and they would reject me.

At one point, I was engaged to a girl who was from a terrible and very unstable family background. Five days before our wedding, she went off and married someone else. I was totally caught off guard as I thought we had a good relationship! Why would she do this? Oh yeah, I forgot I am a reject! At that time, I didn't realize it, but this would lead to a turning point in my life. A few days after she left me, I did something very stupid to get her to feel sorry for me. I tried to scare her into coming back to me. I thought that if I did something dramatic, it would convince her to leave him and come back to me.

My father was taking prescription sleeping pills to help him sleep. I stole several of them from his room and met with my fiancé. While I tried to convince her to come back to me, I downed a handful of them with beer; without realizing it, I had taken enough to kill me. I passed out while talking to her. She assumed I was faking it and loaded me into her car, drove to my best friend John's house, and pulled me out of her car onto the sidewalk in front of his house before driving away.

John just happened to look out his front window and saw me lying there. He knew something was very wrong because I never got that drunk. He dragged me into the house and laid me on his living room floor. As he did, some of the sleeping pills I had left in my pocket fell out onto the floor. John called his next-door neighbor, who was a nurse. She came over, and they tried to wake me up. They rushed me to the county hospital, where they pumped my stomach out. I remember waking up briefly and seeing two police officers standing at the foot of the emergency room bed I was in. I was in a coma for three days. When I woke up, I found myself in the psychiatric ward of the hospital. Over the next few days, the reality that I had almost died hit me, and for the first time, I really wanted to live and find out what life was about. I began to think thoughts like, *Is there more to life than what I see?* and *Is there life after death?* My near-death experience triggered a new curiosity in my life. This began my search for truth.

During this time, I had college friends who were smoking marijuana. At that time, I was a police science major. I had classes where they had us watch movies showing people acting in very bizarre ways after smoking marijuana. This bothered me because none of my friends who were smoking it were acting like that. So, I decided that if I was going to arrest people for this, I ought to find out what it was really like. This was my entry into the world of drugs.

Before long, I became involved with a group of hippies whose lives were centered around weekend get-togethers to go on drug trips. The group was made up of married couples and singles ages nineteen to twenty-five. For the first time, I felt that I was accepted for just being me. The hippie movement was going strong in California at this time, and the emphasis was on "make love, not war." You didn't have to fit the accepted establishment image to be accepted. We identified ourselves by taking on the dress and language of this new subculture.

Soon we all moved into a house together and called ourselves "The Family." We supported our drug habit by buying from high-level drug dealers and selling to the fast-growing circle of college-age kids who were drawn to our group, including my younger brother, Harold. We decided that our goal in life was to buy a sailing yacht and sail around the world together and get away from the rat race, materialistic world that we saw in America. To accomplish this, we decided to put all our salaries into one pot and each take an allowance of five dollars a week. This way, we could save up for the yacht in one year. I was working in construction after dropping out of college and was making good money.

During this time, my involvement with drugs took on a different focus. I began to think that specific drugs could lead me to discover the true meaning of life. I started experimenting regularly with hallucinogenic drugs like LSD, mescaline, and other mind-altering drugs. I read books about people who had spiritual experiences while on drugs that supposedly led them to find the ultimate truth. My search eventually led me to two revelations. One, that there was life after death, and two, that being straight (free from drugs) was the highest high you could experience. I remember one time I was on a drug trip, and I was standing in the living room of a vacation house in the Santa Cruz mountains. My attention was drawn to the bricks that made up the fireplace. As I just kept staring at them, the thought came into my mind that reality was the highest high you could have. Because of this, I began to cut way back on my use of drugs.

Then disaster struck The Family. Without anyone knowing it, the oldest couple in the group had been stealing the money we were saving and spending it on themselves. When we found out about it, there was none left. We had prided ourselves on the fact that we were different from the rest of society and loved one another. This not only shattered our dream of sailing around the world but our hope for a new utopia and trust in people who we thought were our friends. The Family was instantly dissolved, and some who had been lifelong friends now had become bitter enemies. For me, this was just another confirmation that there was no such thing as real love. Maybe you are like how I was and are searching for love and identity. Keep reading on to discover the real love and identity that comes from knowing Jesus!

Chapter Two

MOUNTAIN TOP ENCOUNTER

About this time, I was offered a job opportunity working in Lake Tahoe, Nevada, on a construction crew, building a new hotel. Living in Lake Tahoe was every Californian's dream. I took the job and rented a room in Crystal Bay, the north shore of Lake Tahoe. In my spare time, I would sit in front of the mirror, asking questions like, *"Who am I?" "What's life really about?"* and *"What is the purpose of life?"* I had a strange feeling that something special was about to happen to me. I thought that I was about to meet the girl of my dreams. I felt a sense of destiny.

Sure enough, a short time later, I met a girl named Cheryl, who was a blackjack dealer in one of the casinos on the north shore of the lake. She was living alone with her two daughters. Her husband had deserted her seven years earlier, and she had never seen him since. She was going to college, getting a teaching degree, and the casino was the best paying job she could find to pay her way through. I was attracted to her and started dating her. Each time I took her out, we always ended up in the same argument. She would tell me that what I needed was Jesus, and I would tell her she needed to try LSD. It turns out that Cheryl had been dating a Baptist minister before me, and he had led her to Jesus.

The argument went on for weeks. Cheryl kept on telling me I needed Jesus, and I kept telling her she needed to try LSD. But one thing I couldn't deny was that there was something about her that was different from any girl I'd ever met before. She had a sense of peace and security about her that I had never experienced. Also, she told me about strange miracles that happened to her, like the milk carton in her refrigerator that never ran out of milk.

Finally, one Saturday night, we were having the same argument again, and she said something that I couldn't argue with. "Fred, you have tried everything else. Why don't you try Jesus?" She was right, I had tried to find happiness in so many ways, and they were all dead ends. I didn't know if God really existed but thought it couldn't hurt to find out. So, I decided that the very next day, I would drive up into the mountains and talk to God.

It was a beautiful sunny day. I woke up early and took care of my week's laundry. Around 10 a.m., I drove up into the mountains to find the right spot to talk to God. In my search for answers, I had read a book about supernatural encounters, and one of the things that was emphasized was finding the right spot. I drove up to a forest area that overlooked the lake. I got out of the car and walked up into the woods until I found a place that felt right. I sat down and looked down at the lake. I thought to myself, *Something had to have created all this. It couldn't have just happened by chance.*

I looked up and said, "God, if you're really real, show me, and if Jesus really was your Son, show me that too." Suddenly, I was pressed down against the ground by an unseen force, and a voice started talking to me. The strange thing was that it wasn't an audible voice but strong mental impressions. They were so powerful it was as if I was hearing them with my physical ears. I began crying and sobbing, with thick tears pouring down my face. I realized that if God was real, then I was really messed up. I had never thought about the things I was doing as sin, but now, in the presence of God, the realization of my uncleanness was overwhelming.

He was trying to communicate something to me, but I wasn't getting the message. I thought, *Am I supposed to be part of a special group of people who would bring salvation to the world?* I kept asking questions, but it wasn't becoming any clearer to me. Suddenly, I was picked straight up off the ground and began being dragged down the mountain. I had both heels dug into the ground, but my resistance was futile. It felt like someone had a hold of my wrists, but I couldn't see anyone. I was pulled back down to the road where my car was parked and then over to a newly constructed summer home near it that I hadn't noticed before. Now at this point, you might think I was just having a hallucination from my drug past but let me reassure you that it was real. I even went back later with my wife, Pam, and took pictures of every part of the experience just to prove it really happened.

Next, I found myself standing in front of the entrance to the house. The voice said to me, "Knock on the door." I thought, *No way! If someone comes to the door, they will have me arrested, thinking some crazy hippie drug addict has lost it.* Before I realized it, my arm went up, and I was knocking on the door. A guy wearing a t-shirt, shorts, and tennis shoes answered the door. He said, "Yeah, man, what do you want?" I just stood there with my mouth open, and a voice came out of me and said, "I'm looking for God." Without any sign that he thought that it was a strange question, he answered, "I'm sorry, He's not here." This answered something that I was trying to understand about this encounter. I thought before that I was to be a part of some special group, but I now realized that this just had to do with me. This was something personal between God and me.

As I thought about this, I walked back to my car and was leaning against it crying when I noticed that the young man who had answered the door had come out of the house and was getting into his car. There was a girl with him. I believe they were angels because they acted like they understood what was happening to me. The Bible says that we are to be hospitable to strangers as we might be entertaining angels. He backed the car over to where I was and motioned for me to follow him. The voice I had been hearing said, "Get in your car and follow him." So, I got in and started the car and put it into gear, and it took off. On one side of the road, there was the mountain, and on the other, a cliff that dropped off a thousand feet. All kinds of things were racing through my mind like: *This is what happens to people just before they die, and I'm about to die*, and *Someone is using some kind of mind control on me. Maybe some witches or something.* I followed the car, but I put both feet on the brake and slowed my car down out of fear.

Soon I found myself at a fork in the road. I didn't see which way the car went, so I took the left fork. I went a little way, and the voice said, "You're going the wrong way; turn around." I turned the car around and went in the other direction. Soon I came upon another mountain cabin on the left-hand side of the road. It was very strange looking. It was built into two modules that were in a hexagon shape. In the middle was a breezeway that was the entry to the cabin. As I passed by, the voice said to me, "That's the house." I said, "That's the house?" And the voice repeated itself. So, I stopped the car and pulled into the driveway. As soon as I got out of the car, I was physically taken over again and led into the entry of the house.

When I got to the entry door, the voice said to me, "Knock on the door." I knew that I would be made to do it anyway, so I knocked. I waited, trembling with fear of what or who would answer the door. Finally, I realized that no one was there. I looked up and said, "There's no one there." The voice immediately said, "Try the door." So, I reached out and tried the door. It was locked. I looked up and said, "The door is locked." Then the voice said to me, "The door is Jesus Christ." Suddenly, I understood for the first time in my life that Jesus Christ was the Son of God and that He is alive. Cheryl had been trying to tell me that Jesus was the way to God, and I wasn't hearing it. I knew that He was the door to get to God, the Father. A month later, when I was reading in the Gospel of John, chapter 10, I discovered that Jesus said that He was the door to the sheepfold. I also read in John, chapter 14, that Jesus said that He was the only way to God, the Father. Now I knew that the voice was God answering my question. He was showing me that Jesus was the way to come to know Him. I felt a heavy weight lift off my shoulders. It wasn't until sometime later that I understood that it was the weight of my guilt, shame, and sins.

My first reaction was, "I've got to tell someone about this." So, I started to go out to my car, and I was physically brought back into the entryway. I felt a pressure on my head pushing downward, so I laid down on the concrete. Then I felt a pressure pulling me up, and I stood up. This happened a few more times until I got on my knees. This is where God wanted me. He said to me, "From now on, you're working for Me. Then he said to me, "Go find a church." There was something different about the voice now. It was coming from inside of me instead of from the outside.

I felt the pressure holding me begin to lift, so I got in my car and drove to the nearest phone booth to call

Cheryl. When she answered the phone, I said, "You won't believe what just happened to me! God just talked to me!" She said, "That's great." I realized she wasn't really understanding what I meant. I said, "You don't understand; He literally talked to me." She said, "That's great; you should go talk to someone at a church." I told her I'd talk to her later and hung up. I got back in my car and drove to my friend's summer cabin to rest and reflect on what had just happened to me.

While I was there, God's voice inside of me kept saying, "Go find a church, go find a church." It kept getting stronger and stronger. Finally, I realized I needed to respond. I drove to a nearby gas station and asked the attendant where the nearest church was. I told him I didn't care what brand it was. He pointed down a street and told me about a new Baptist church nearby. I drove to it and got out of my car and walked up to the front door, and looked in the window. It was seven o'clock, and the evening service had just begun. I saw the people inside, and none of them looked like me. I was wearing buckskin clothes with fringes that had beads on them. I looked up and said, "I can't go in there." The Lord spoke to me and said, "The door is always open; go on in."

I went into the church and stood in the back. They were singing hymns. A little girl about eight years old held up her hymn book, so I could follow along. It brought tears to my eyes. When they finished singing, the pastor preached his Sunday night message. He spoke about the Apostle Paul's conversion to Christ. Saul, whose name later was changed to Paul, was traveling on the road to Damascus to persecute the Christians when a light from the sky flashed around him, and he heard a voice speaking to him. The voice said, "Saul, Saul, why do you persecute me?" Saul answered, "Who are you, Lord?" The voice said, "I am Jesus, whom you are persecuting." Saul was blinded by the light and had to be led away to a house in Damascus. He was blind for three days, and the Lord sent a man named Ananias to pray for him to be filled with the Spirit and receive his sight.

As the pastor spoke, I found myself relating to Paul's experience. I, too, had God speak to me. I, too, was blind, not physically but spiritually. I was blind to the reality of God's existence and the knowledge that Jesus Christ was His Son. And not only that, but that He had risen from the dead. He was alive! Paul had come to the same realization I had, "Jesus is the Savior of the world, and He cares about us individually."

The pastor finished his message and asked if there was anyone who had a testimony. I had no idea what a testimony was. The only testimony I knew of was when I testified before a judge and was put in jail. In response to the pastor's question, three people stood up and shared how they had become Christians. One was a construction worker who was led to Christ by some fellow workers during a lunch break. Another was a man who had become a believer while he was on a hunting trip. The third was a housewife who had been introduced to Jesus through a neighbor. None of them had the radical experience that I had. But that didn't make any difference because they all came to the same conclusion: that Jesus is the risen Son of God and He's alive!

After they finished, the pastor looked right at me and asked if anyone else had anything else to say. I thought to myself, well, why not. So, I stood up and told them what had happened to me in every detail. As I finished, people started crying and weeping all over the congregation. They all got up and came and surrounded me. The pastor put his arm around me and told me I had been born again. I said, "Oh, is that what it is?" He gave me a Gideons Bible and wrote on the front, "Fred Kropp, born again, April 6, 1970."

I didn't even know what a Gideons Bible was. During the next year, I was asked to speak at several churches because of my testimony of being a former drug addict. People would look at me funny when I walked into the church. They thought, *Hey, that guy stole the Bible out of the motel.* Well, it was my Bible, and I loved it.

Maybe you haven't come to the place where you know that Jesus is alive and that He is the Messiah, the Son of the Living God. It was an act of obedience by a young woman named Cheryl that brought me to the place of encountering God's salvation through Jesus Christ. I challenge you like Cheryl challenged me. Why don't you try Jesus? You have nothing to lose and eternal life to gain. Ask God right now to reveal His Son to you. He is waiting for you to ask Him.

Chapter Three

I'VE GOT TO TELL SOMEONE

I left the church that night and went right to one of the casinos. I walked into one of the dinner shows and went from table to table, telling people about my encounter with God. I would sit down at their table and say, "Guess what happened to me today?" I told them that God just spoke to me on the mountain, and I found out that He was real and that Jesus was His Son. I was so filled with the excitement of this experience that I didn't even stop to think of what the people that I sat down with would think of some hippie guy trying to talk to them, telling them some crazy story. Maybe they thought I was a part of the show. What was amazing was that they would listen intently to me. Some of them would start crying while I talked. They seemed to respond positively to what I was telling them. Some even shared their own experiences with God. I remember one young man who was there with his girlfriend. After I shared what had happened to me, he began to cry and tell me about an encounter he had with God when he was

37

a soldier in Vietnam. I thought, *Hey, people really like this.* I think part of the reason that people were reacting so positively was that the glory of God was on me. I had just spent several hours in the very presence of God, and I was shining with His presence. Later that year, when I spoke at churches and Christian events, people would come up to me and tell me my face was shining. Then I got my first negative response. After going from table to table, I thought, *I've got to call my mother,* who was back in San Jose, and tell her what had happened to me. When she answered, I began telling her what had just happened to me. She said, "Fritz [my nickname], you need to come home. You are tired and need to rest." I tried to tell her that this really happened, and she wasn't buying it. She said, "Son, you need to see a psychiatrist." I'm pretty sure that she probably thought that I had overdosed on drugs and blown my mind. Realizing that I wasn't getting through to her, I hung up the phone.

Three days later, the Lord told me to quit my construction job there in Lake Tahoe and go home to San Jose and tell my friends about Him. I submitted my resignation the next day and headed for home. On the way, I stopped by Cheryl's house in Pollock Pines, California. Cheryl was the girl who had told me I needed to try Jesus. I told her all the details of my encounter with God. My experience was a little too radical for her, and she wasn't sure if this was the genuine thing.

I arrived back in San Jose on a Saturday morning. I went to the house where I used to live with my hippie friends. I found my brother, Harold, who was three years younger than me, and several of my close friends loading their cars with camping gear. I asked them what they were doing. They informed me that they had formed a search party to go to Lake Tahoe and find me. They figured I had overdosed on drugs and blown my mind. My mother told my brother about my phone call and that I was running through the woods in Tahoe, naked with my head shaved. (I have no idea how she got that out of our conversation.) She told him to go find me and bring me back.

There were about ten or twelve of my friends standing there looking at me. I said, "You won't believe what happened to me." As I told them about my experience, they all stood together in a group about fifteen feet away and nodded their heads and said things like, "You'll be all right," and "Don't come any closer to us!" I was right; they didn't believe me. In fact, they were all convinced that I had overdosed on drugs, lost my mind, and would attack them at any minute. I lost all my friends at one time. None of them wanted to be around me anymore because all I could talk about was Jesus and try to convince them to believe too. Here was rejection again but for a different reason. This time it was about my belief in a resurrected Jesus.

Because of my newfound revelation that God was real and that heaven and hell were a reality, I didn't want any of my friends or family to end up in hell. I was especially concerned about my best friend, Dan. I would go over to his house and knock on the door. I could hear him say to his mother, "If it is Fred, tell him I am not here." My own family thought I was crazy as well. My mother would follow me around the house, yelling, "You're crazy, you're crazy!" One of my cousins, Larry, who had considered becoming a priest in the Catholic church when he was younger, told me I needed to back off with the Jesus stuff. I witnessed this to my family and friends over and over for six months, and no one gave their life to Jesus. I was so frustrated that I remember throwing myself down on the lawn in our front yard and yelling at God, "What do I have to do to see them get saved?" He spoke to me and said, "Get as close to Me as you can, and as you do, it will form a net behind you that will catch them." I determined to not say anything about Jesus to them. It was hard not to.

Then I experienced my first new convert. I called my best friend, Dan, on the phone one day. At that time, he was living with his girlfriend. I just talked about how he was doing and other things. Then just before we hung up, I said, "Dan, you wouldn't want to get saved, would you?" He said, "Yes, I would." It went right by me as I was used to hearing no as an answer. I started to hang up the phone and realized Dan had just said he wanted to get saved. I said, "Right now?" And he said, "Yes." So, I prayed with him right on the phone to receive Jesus. As soon as he hung up the phone, he turned to his girlfriend and told her she was going to have to move out because he was a Christian now. She was so angry with me that she went looking for me to beat me up. While she was looking, she encountered the Lord herself and gave her life to Him too. After this, Dan led sixty of my friends to Jesus over the next three months.

I didn't understand why they didn't accept Jesus from my witnessing to them. I probably came on too strong. Dan was much more persuasive in sharing the Gospel with them. He knew how to disarm their roadblocks and arguments to the Gospel, but I must take some credit for their salvations. I learned later from the Apostle Paul's words in his letter to the church at Corinth that one plants and another waters. He said, "I planted, Apollos watered, but God was causing the growth." I planted the seed of the Gospel; Dan watered the seed, and God caused it to take root and grow.

This became very real to me several years later when I was taking a flight from Milwaukee, Wisconsin, to Kansas City, Missouri. I had several of my flights canceled because of bad weather and was stuck in Milwaukee overnight. I was frustrated and angry at God because I had only a couple of days at home before I had to fly out on another trip again. Finally, a flight opened up the next day to get me home. I boarded my plane and was sitting in my seat when my attention was drawn to a very large and very drunk man who was coming down the aisle. He had a shaggy-looking beard and was dressed like a lumberjack. He reminded me of Paul Bunyan. He was well over six feet tall. As he staggard down the aisle, he was talking very loudly, bumping into people as he came. I looked at him and thought, *I feel sorry for the poor person he is going to be sitting next to.* Yup, you guessed it! It was me.

He plopped down in the seat next to me and turned to me, and said in a loud voice, "I want to talk!" Being the brave guy that I am, I said in a wimpy sounding voice, "Okay." He told me his name was Bill. As I sat there looking up at Bill, he began to tell me what a mean and tough guy he was. He told me that one time he found his wife in a bar with a couple of guys. He said that he knocked out one of them with a cue ball from a pool table and threw the other guy through the plate glass window in the front of the bar. I decided I should say something, and so I asked him what he was doing in Milwaukee. He told me he had come there because his ten-year-old nephew had asked him if he would ever come and take him fishing. When he said it, his voice started to crack with emotion.

Then I did something that I knew might cause me to be severely beaten or at least physically harmed. I put my finger right in the middle of Bill's chest (thinking I would never see this finger again) and said, "Bill, you need Jesus!" To my shock, Bill broke down crying. (Whew, that was close.) He went on to tell me that some guy he worked with at his job had been talking to him about Jesus and had given him a Bible. He said that he had been reading it every night. Well, I led Bill to Jesus right there on the plane, and he immediately changed. He went from very drunk to immediately sober. His whole attitude changed, and he became very happy, humble, and friendly. When we landed in Kansas City, his elderly mother was waiting at the baggage claim to pick him up. He dragged me over to her and said, "Mom, I want you to meet this preacher that led me to Jesus." Sometimes an act of obedience requires taking a risk. I didn't want to talk with Bill when he sat down next to me. I certainly didn't want to put my finger in his chest, knowing I was risking at the very least a punch in the face. But I knew that Bill sitting next to me was no accident. God had changed the weather for one man to give his life to Jesus. I understood that it was preplanned by God, and that gave me the courage to take the risk. Someone else had been planting the seed of the Gospel, and I came along and watered it, and God caused it to take root and bring salvation to Bill.

You never know what your one act of obedience is going to produce. You may be just planting a seed or watering a seed that has already been planted. You may or may not see the results right then. But know that your one act of obedience is making an eternal difference in someone's life and for God's kingdom.

Chapter Four

A WOMAN NAMED AMY AND A MAN NAMED BILL

When I was a young child, a neighbor lady named Amy Piedmont would babysit me. Her son, Johnny, was one of my best friends at school. She and her husband, Bill, were close friends with my parents. They used to party together all the time. Amy was known in our neighborhood for being the wildest woman at the parties. During the parties, she could dance, drink bourbon, and smoke cigars all at the same time. That was wild back in the fifties. One day my mother came home from visiting Amy and said, "That Amy is no fun anymore, she's got religion!" This was my mother's take on Amy getting saved. What my mom said meant nothing to me. I had no idea what she was talking about. Amy's life had done a complete one hundred and eighty-degree turnaround.

One morning when I was a freshman in high school, I was walking past her house on the way to school. Amy came out of her house into the middle of the street and grabbed my arm. She started saying something about me needing God and was trying to put some little booklet in my hand. (It was a Christian tract that explained the Gospel.) I looked at her and said, "Amy, you are a fanatic!" and ran down the street away from her, determined never to walk that way to school again. And I never did!

Now at twenty-two years of age, I found myself with no family or friends that could relate to me in my new relationship with Jesus. Who was I going to talk to; who would believe me? Then I remembered Amy. I decided to go and pay her a visit. The thing I didn't know was that her son, Johnny, who was in Vietnam during the war, had gotten hooked on heroin. Amy blamed her son's addiction on the hippie drug culture. Now here I am, a hippie Christian; it would be a challenge for Amy to want to have anything to do with me.

Here I stood knocking at Amy's door, dressed in a buckskin jacket and beads. Only now, I had a new item, a big wooden cross hanging around my neck. When she opened the door, I said, "Hi Amy, I'm a fanatic too." She took two steps back and looked at me for a few moments, and finally got enough courage to invite me in. We sat at her kitchen table, and I told her about my encounter with God on the side of the mountain. I told her about how I had come to believe in Jesus and how He had changed my life. As I shared with her, she began to cry, telling me that the Holy Spirit was witnessing with her spirit that this was the real thing. She called her pastor and asked him to come right over and hear my story. He showed up a little while later. Amy said to him, "You won't believe Fred's story." I shared my testimony with him, and Amy was right; he didn't believe it and left as quickly as he had come. But Amy believed in me and was willing to lay down her life to help me grow in God.

Over the next several months, I would go to Amy's house every day after work and sit at her dining room table and share with her what the Lord was doing in my life. Some of the things I would come up with were biblically off. She would show me scriptures in the Bible to correct and to help me, and then she would pray for me. At one point, I believed I needed to join the Mormon church. When I told Amy, she freaked out and told me that they were a cult and that they didn't believe in the same Jesus that we did. I wasn't sure I believed her. I contacted them and asked them to send some of their missionaries to my house. Now I lived on a main street in San Jose, and my house was very easy to find. They sent missionaries twice to my house, and they could not find it. The Lord had blinded their eyes in answer to Amy's prayers which were protecting me.

Amy discipled me and grounded me in the foundations of the Christian life. I owe a great debt to her! She sacrificed her own time with her family to help this hippie Christian get to know Jesus. If it wasn't for Amy Piedmont, I wouldn't be where I am today. Lord, give us more people like Amy Piedmont to disciple new believers!

One of the things I told Amy was, "No church!" She

said, "What do you mean?" I said, "Don't try to get me to go to your church!" I told her this was because none of my high school friends who went to church ever told me about Jesus. I believed that Jesus and church didn't go together. One day Amy tricked me into going to her church. She told me there was a meeting at her church on Saturday and that it wasn't church. And I believed her. It was church. When I went to the meeting, I could feel the presence of God and even saw angels flying through the building during the service. So, I was in. From then on, every time the church doors were opened, I was there. I was the first hippie Christian the church had ever experienced.

My being there created a few issues for the church. For one, I didn't know how church worked or that there was an order for the services. They would have testimony times on Wednesday nights. When I learned about testimonies, I thought it meant that any time you thought of something Jesus had done for you, you were to stand up and tell everyone about it. Well, Jesus was doing things in my life all the time. I would stand up at any time in the service, even in the middle of the pastor's Sunday message. I would jump up and say, "Pastor Johnson, that is a great message, but I just want to tell one more thing Jesus did for me this week." This was starting to concern some of the church members.

Sometime later, Pastor Johnson moved on to another church, and we got a new pastor. He was very familiar with what the Lord was doing with the hippies and what was now being called the "Jesus People Movement."

He saw what the Lord was doing in my life and decided to make me the youth leader in the church. This really concerned several of the parents because they had been saying, "That hippie drug addict has got our kids!"

One Wednesday night, I was unable to attend the service, and some of the parents used the opportunity to express their concerns about me being the church youth leader. In the meeting was a long-term member of the church named Bill Wallace, who was a high school counselor. He stood up and rebuked the church for their attitude toward me, which I wasn't even aware of. I loved them all and believed they all loved me.

Soon after that, Bill asked me if I would invite unsaved teenagers and young adults to come to his house to hear about Jesus. I said yes. The first week we invited four young adults over to Bill's house. Two of them were Christians, and two were not. We put the four of them in a room together and let them talk. The results were that we now had four believers in Jesus. The next week we invited four more unbelievers and put them in a room with the four believers, and now we had six followers of Jesus. Two more had received Him as their Savior. Over the next two months, the number grew to 250 young people filling every inch of space in Bill's house. They were sitting on the living room floor, in the kitchen, down the hallway, into the bedrooms, and even into the bathroom. We would be sitting there in our meeting, and a knock would come at the door. When we opened it, there would be some kid standing there saying, "I don't know what you have going on here, but I want it!" And they would be saved.

Think of it. This all began with one woman named Amy and her one act of obedience when she walked out into the street to tell me that I needed God. You never know what the full impact of your one act of obedience might have. Never think that your one act of obedience is insignificant or a waste of time. You could be planting the seeds of the Gospel in the next Billy Graham or Reinhart Bonnke, who was probably the world's greatest evangelist and preached the Gospel to crowds of up to a million people in a single meeting. Or it might be a David Yonggi Cho, who was the pastor of the world's largest church in Seoul, Korea. He was led to Jesus by a young Christian girl who came to his home when he was in bed dying from tuberculosis. There is one act of obedience waiting for you today that will change someone's life forever.

Chapter Five

HE WHO FINDS A WIFE!

"He who finds a wife finds a good thing, and obtains favor from the LORD" (Proverbs 18:22).

As I learned about being a follower of Jesus, I soon discovered that the way you receive things from Him was through prayer. At the very top of my prayer list was, "I need a wife!" Well, to be honest, I probably only had one thing on the list, and that was it. I also learned that other Christians could join you in your prayer requests. So, I went to every Christian I knew and asked them to be praying for me to find a wife. Almost all my reasons and motives for wanting a wife were selfish and fleshly. But I was desperate! I kept bugging my Christian friends to make sure they were praying about it.

I was at the beach one day and found a ring in the sand and thought, whoever this ring fits, was going to be my wife. The problem was it was a common-sized ladies' ring that fits most girls. Yeah, that was dumb! Over time, wanting to be married became more important than my relationship with the Lord. I realized I had to die to it. So, I gave up looking.

Not long after I did this, I was the guest speaker to the youth at an all-district church camp meeting in the Santa Cruz mountains. The day I was going to be speaking, a friend from the church I was attending came up to me with a girl named Pam Caswell. Pam was home from college for the summer. She was going to a Nazarene Church College in Idaho, called Northwest Nazarene College or NNC. Pam had a younger sister, Patty, who was doing drugs. A friend of mine had shared my testimony with Pam, and she wanted to ask me how she could help her sister. I don't remember what I told her or how helpful I was.

Later that night, when I finished speaking, my friend John, Amy's son, said, "Hey, let's go get pizza with a group of us." I turned around, and there was Pam standing nearby. I asked her if she wanted to go with us and she said yes. She and I began spending time together every day. Our dates would consist of us going out witnessing about Jesus or preaching in rescue missions or going to Jesus' People meetings.

We were sitting on the front porch of her father's house one day, and I was telling her how I needed to go to Bible college but couldn't figure out how to afford it. Then I came up with a brilliant idea. I said, "I know; let's get married, and you can work while I attend Bible college."

Then we started laughing, and I said, "Did I just propose to you?" She said, "Yeah, I guess you did."

After that, I went to my pastor and told him what I had said, and he thought marrying Pam was from the Lord. We had only known each other for two whole weeks. The next thing I did was go to Pam's father and ask him if it was alright for me to marry her. He told me that the first time he met me, he knew that I would be Pam's husband.

At the end of the two weeks, Pam went back to college in Idaho. Before she left, we made an agreement that if for any reason we felt that God would say no to us getting married, we would let go of it. We set the wedding date to be three months later when she came home for Christmas break. While Pam was back in Idaho and I was in California, we wrote letters to each other practically every day. (Letters were like emails or texts written on paper, I know you needed to know that.) What was amazing was that as our letters to each other crossed in the mail, we would be sharing the same Scriptures that the Lord was showing each of us.

About a month and a half into our engagement, I felt the Lord telling me that I was to move to San Francisco and join a ministry in the Haight Ashbury district. Haight Ashbury was known as the central hippy culture area. The ministry was called "The Clayton House." It was made up of former hippies who had been converted to Christ. It was a very powerful ministry that carried a strong presence of the Lord and was reaching a lot of young hippie people. One of the requirements of this ministry was that you couldn't be married while serving there. I couldn't believe the Lord was asking me to give up my right to be married at this time and break off my engagement with Pam.

I went to every spiritually mature Christian I knew and told them what the Lord was asking me to do, hoping that they would show me a way out of it. Fortunately, they were mature, and they all said that they wouldn't touch it with a ten-foot pole. (Translation: If God is telling you to do something, we cannot tell you to do anything but obey Him.) I made an appointment to meet with the pastor of my church on Saturday morning, thinking he would know a way for me to get out of this.

I arrived early to find the church doors opened because the janitor was cleaning the church. The pastor hadn't arrived yet. So, I walked into the sanctuary and sat on one of the front pews. As I sat there, I wrestled in my mind struggling with the thought of giving up what I had prayed so long for! As I sat there, I noticed a square wooden box sitting on the floor in front of the pulpit. It was four feet long, three feet wide, and about three feet high. It had the letters, INRI, carved into the front of it. INRI, the words that were written above the head of Jesus when He hung on the cross. INRI meant, "Jesus the Nazarene King of the Jews." I had no idea what they stood for. This box is where they placed the communion trays for the communion services. I didn't know that either. I just thought that this is the place where people go forward and offer themselves as a living sacrifice to the Lord.

Finally, I gave up my struggle and said yes to the Lord! I

said, "I give up my right to be married to obey what You're asking me to do!" I stood up from the pew I was sitting on and went and laid down on the INRI box, offering myself as a living sacrifice. As soon as I laid down, the Lord said to me, "This was just a test, and you passed it." Wow, was I relieved! Of course, this wasn't the only time God would ask me to give up my rights. Most of the future tests weren't just a test; they were for real! I had to let go of what I wanted and submit to what He wanted. Can I say at this point that I have never regretted saying yes to the Lord, even though dying to self was painful? Saying yes to the Lord has always led to greater fruitfulness, greater fulfillment, and bigger adventures with Jesus!

A month and a half later, Pam and I were married, and we moved to Idaho for her to finish college and for us to start our new adventure together. Little did we know that a major part of the adventure was learning what marriage was about and learning to love someone who was almost the total opposite of yourself. But that is another story for another time.

I began this chapter with "*He who* finds a wife finds a good *thing* and obtains favor from the LORD" (Proverbs 18:22). Pam and I have been married for over fifty years! When I found Pam, actually the Lord found her for me, I found more than a good thing! I found a partner in Jesus! I found a woman with the gift of faith! I found a person who loves Jesus with all her heart and loves to worship Him! I found a woman who gives herself selflessly to help others! I found someone who has always encouraged and believed in me! I found a Christian who was excited about sharing and demonstrating Jesus and His kingdom with total strangers. Over the years, we have been through both amazing and trying times, and she has stood with me in the face of giants that we encountered along the way. She has always believed the best about me and everyone she has met! Truly a woman of God with one main goal in life, to hear the Lord say, "Well done, good and faithful servant!" when she meets Him face to face. She has been an example to me of what it means to be a true disciple of Jesus. I honor her for all she is and has done and will do for Jesus and His kingdom.

Chapter Six

GOD VISITS A COLLEGE

It was the last three months of the school year at Northwest Nazarene College. My wife, Pam, was a student there, and I was working at a Swiss Colony Cheese Store. The Lord started doing some things in my life that made no sense to me. He would wake me up each morning and start giving me specific instructions for the day. He would give me a series of things that I was to specifically carry out. For example, He would say, "Get up, make your bed, get dressed, go outside, turn right, walk a hundred steps, and there will be someone there, that you know, I want you to talk to that you know." Sure enough, it would happen exactly as the Lord had said. Each day He would give me a different set of instructions. Each time I would walk them out no matter how strange they seemed. This went on for two months. What I didn't realize was that He was training me to hear just one command. He made sure that I wouldn't miss it and that I would obey whatever He said.

It was about two weeks before the end of the school year, and I was waiting for Pam in the side wing of the large church on campus. It was there they had their weekly chapel service. Suddenly, the Lord spoke to me and said, "I want you to hold a meeting on campus next Tuesday at 1 p.m." I said, "Is this really You, Lord?" He repeated the message. I asked a third time, and He repeated it again. I was now convinced that it was the Lord. As the chapel service was just ending, I spotted the student body president and told him what God had just said to me. He said, "You'll have to get permission for the meeting." I said, "Who do I talk to?" He said, "Dr. DuBois" (pronounced "do-boys"). Dr. DuBois was the head of the religion department and school chaplain.

I walked out the front entry to go find Dr. DuBois and ran right into him. "Dr. DuBois," I said, "I was just on the way to talk to you." I told him that God had spoken to me and that I wanted to hold a meeting on campus next Tuesday at 1 p.m. I could tell by the look on his face that he wasn't for the idea. He said, "What's the purpose of the meeting?" Before I had time to think, I responded bluntly, "When God tells me to do something, I don't ask Him what the purpose is!" His head snapped back as if I had slapped him in the face. When he recovered, he said, "All right, let's do it." It was as if God had changed his mind whether he wanted it changed or not.

As soon as I finished talking with Dr. DuBois, I realized I would need a sound system for the meeting. I literally turned around from talking with Dr. DuBois, and standing right in front of me was John McClees. John was a student at the college who owned a sound system that he rented out to music groups. I told him about the meeting and my need for a sound system. He said, "No problem, you got it. I'll have it there for you."

As I finished with John, I knew the next thing I needed to do was to get the word out. I needed some advertising. Where would I get that? I looked up, and I was standing right near the office building that both the student newspaper and the college radio station were in. I went upstairs to the radio studio, and a student I knew was currently on the air. I went in and told him my need, and he said they would announce it every hour. I thanked him and walked over to the newspaper office and told them about the meeting, and they said that the paper was going out in the next few days and that they would put an announcement in it about the meeting. What was amazing about all this was that I looked at my watch, and it had only been ten to fifteen minutes since the Lord had told me to hold the meeting. I had permission, a sound system, and advertising on radio and in the newspaper. The only thing I didn't have was any idea what the meeting was for or what was to happen at it.

When Tuesday morning came, I woke up and was struck with fear. All weekend long, I was so busy that I hadn't read my Bible or prayed about this meeting that was scheduled for 1 p.m. that day. I started to panic when the Lord spoke in my spirit, "Read Hebrews 11." I opened Hebrews 11, which is the faith chapter in the Bible, and got the message, "Trust Me!" The Lord was telling me to believe Him and trust Him for the results. What was about to happen wasn't going to be the result of any good works of mine. A few years ago, I heard a message by Dr. David Yonggi Cho on how to see miracles take place in your life. There was one statement he made that was life-changing for me. He said, "Only God can work the works of God." Our part is to trust and obey. For faith to work, it must be accompanied by acts of obedience. James 2:18–20 says faith without works is dead or useless. I didn't understand it then, but my act of obeying the voice of God was about to release a major outpouring of His Spirit on the college.

At 1 p.m., I walked out to the grass area in the middle of the campus where the meeting was to be held. There was the sound system just like John had promised. I looked around, and there was no one in sight. I thought, *I guess no one is coming*. Then students started coming from all directions. Five, ten, twenty, fifty, a hundred, two hundred. There were somewhere around 250 students gathered to see what this meeting was all about. They all sat down on the grass and looked at me as if to say, "Alright, we're here. Now what?" I looked up, and here came some of my friends carrying signs exalting Jesus.

I led the crowd in a couple of Jesus' People songs, playing my guitar. Then I said, "Okay, Lord. Now what?" The Lord told me to ask a student I knew to come up and share something the Lord was doing in his life. When he finished, the Lord had me ask another and another until I had called five people to come up and share. While the fifth one was sharing it happened, rain started falling out of a clear blue sky. I am talking about real, wet raindrops. There was not a cloud to be seen anywhere! This was a miracle like the miracles God did through Moses in Egypt. I'm not comparing myself to Moses in any way. Later I discovered in Psalm 68:8 that "the heavens also dropped rain at the presence of God." When the raindrops hit the crowd, many of them dropped to the ground. Some started weeping loudly. Others started yelling, "I repent!" Others were going through deliverance with demons coming out of them with yells and screams. I didn't even know if I believed in the things that were taking place as I had never seen anything like this before.

The next thing I knew, I was going through the crowd, touching and pointing at people, and they were instantly being filled with the Holy Spirit and began speaking in tongues. I was also commanding evil spirits to come out of those who were manifesting demons. What was so unusual was that I had never done anything like this before. I didn't understand much about the baptism of the Holy Spirit and certainly knew nothing about evil spirits. Students were holding each other, crying on each other's shoulders, and praying for one another. Pam and I stayed there for about four hours and then went home. There were several students still there when we left.

About five o'clock, Pam and I had dinner and went to bed. I really had no comprehension of the magnitude of what was taking place. About midnight, we were awakened by our phone ringing.

I answered it only to hear some student, whom I didn't know, yelling, "I've got it, I've got it!"

I asked, "You've got what?"

He said, "I've been saved and filled with the Spirit!"

I said, "That's great."

He said, "It's going through all the dormitories!" I said to him, "Great! I'm trying to sleep here," and hung up the phone with a click. I said to Pam, "I think something's really going on here."

The next day I was waiting for Pam outside the large church building where they held their student chapel services. Dr. Laird, who was over student affairs, came running up and grabbed me by the shirt and started shaking me and yelling, "You've got to stop it! You've got to stop it!" I said, "Stop what?" He said, "It's taking over the whole campus!" I said, "I didn't start it; God did." With that, he ran off with a panicked look on his face. I thought I better get into the chapel service; *something big is about to happen.*

I went into the chapel service and sat in the back of the church. Several of the students were already there. The presence of the Lord was so thick you could cut it with a knife. The building was filled with electricity! I started crying. The chapel that day was to be a sports awards ceremony where they gave out end-of-the-year awards for various sports competitions that had taken place between student groups. The college administrators came in and sat in their large high back chairs on the platform. They all had sort of an unhappy religious look on their faces showing they were very concerned about what was going on. I knew something was about to happen. You could sense the tension in the air.

Dr. Mayfield, the vice president of the college, stood up and started to make his way to the microphone. Before he got to the microphone, one of the students named Mike Rice, who was the editor of the student newspaper, a self-proclaimed atheist, who wrote an anti-Christian column, ran up on the stage and jumped in front of him, grabbing the microphone. Mike shouted into the microphone, "I have been saved!" With that, hundreds of students ran forward and filled the area in front of the platform, falling to their knees, crying. The administrators on the platform quickly turned around and went to their knees in their chairs.

For the next several hours, one student after another came up to the microphone and told how they had been convicted and touched by God. Some even confessed their sins and made a commitment to change their lifestyle. Indeed, God was visiting the college. Everywhere you went around the campus, you saw students talking to others, encouraging them to sell out their lives to Christ. I would walk up to students, and without saying a word to them, they would fall to the ground and start crying. I thought, *Look out, Billy Graham, here comes Fred Kropp.*

The end of the school year came a day or two later, and the students went home for the summer spreading the revival in their home churches. Ten years later, I read an article in the church's denominational magazine by one of the students who were there. It was titled "My Personal Pentecost." He spoke of how the revival was the turning point in his life and that he had never been the same since.

During the two weeks following the end of school, I was in the desert south of Boise doing my two-week summer camp duty with the National Guard. One day, I felt led by the Spirit to walk out into the desert away from our camp. While I was out there, the Lord spoke to me. He said, "I want you to understand something. You had very little to do with what happened at the college." He revealed to me the real cause of this visitation. During the school year, there were small prayer gatherings that had sprung up all over the campus that were asking God to do something about the spiritually dead condition of the students at the college. The Lord said, "What happened was in response to their prayers." He let me know that I was just a pawn that He used to ignite the fire." At that point, I let go of my visions of grandeur and aspirations of replacing Billy Graham.

I remembered one night earlier during the school year, I was in the basement of the college church and heard a noise coming from one of the rooms. I opened the door, and there, lying on their faces on the floor, were several students praying and crying out to God to send an outpouring of His Spirit to the college. Now I understand that the outpouring was in direct response to the intercessions and prayers of God's people. Second Chronicles 7:14, "If My people who are called by My name will humble themselves, and pray and seek My face, and turn from their wicked ways, then I will hear from heaven, forgive their sin and heal their land." Divine appointments are the direct result of prayer. Jesus told His disciples to look at the multitudes and notice that they were sheep without a shepherd, and then He said, "Pray to the Lord of the harvest that He would send forth workers into the harvest." The workers are those who experience divine appointments because of the prayers of God's people.

A week after this experience, the Lord spoke to me and told me that this outpouring was a small example of what He was going to do in California on a massive scale in the future. I believe we are moving into that time now. There have been Christians praying for revival for the last fifty years and especially over the last year and a half. The Lord has heard our prayers and is ready to move. What is required now is for us to hear His voice and be willing to act in one act of obedience! The world is groaning and waiting for the manifestation of the sons and daughters of God. Divine appointments are waiting for you to step into them now!

In conclusion, don't think that you are not making a difference if you don't have some dramatic move of God happen through you. Just know that God is pleased with all your small acts of obedience!

Chapter Seven

HEARING GOD'S VOICE

The Key to One Act of Obedience

Years ago, I was flying back to Kansas City from California. I was at the Ontario, California, airport waiting for my flight and decided to call my wife, Pam. Back then, we didn't have cell phones (I know this sounds ancient), so I had to use the payphone at the airport. At that time, Ontario airport was a small airport, and they only had one payphone. When I got to it, there was a line of six to eight people waiting to use the phone. So, I got in line. As I stood there, I noticed a businessman who was a few people ahead of me. He was wearing a nice sports jacket, blue jeans, and expensive-looking cowboy boots and was carrying an expensive-looking briefcase.

When I looked at him, I heard the Holy Spirit tell me to go and tell him three things. One had to do with his marriage, another with his spiritual life, and the third had to do with God using him in the church. So, I got out of line and walked up to him and said, "Sir, you don't know me, but God just spoke to me and told me to tell you these three things." He looked back at me with the look, "You are an idiot, and you're bothering me!" I told him the three things God had said to me, and he gave me a go-away look. I told him I was just telling him what God told me to tell him. So, I walked back to my place in line, and he made his call and walked away.

Later, when I went to my board my plane to Kansas City, I stepped onto the plane and turned right to go down the aisle, guess who was sitting there in first class. That's right, the businessman from Texas. He looked at me with the look, "Oh no, that nut is on my flight." Well, I wasn't going to say anything to him because I had already told him what God had said. As I passed by him, he grabbed my arm and asked who I was. I told him I was a pastor from Kansas City. He asked me if I had a calling card. I gave him my card and went back to sit in the cattle car section. The flight took us to Dallas, Texas, where he got off and then went onto Kansas City.

About six months or so later, Pam was bringing in our mail and said, "Here is a letter from some man in Dallas." I said, "I don't know any man in Dallas." So, I opened the letter, and it said, "Dear Pastor Fred. Several months ago, I was at Ontario airport, and you walked up to me and told me three things God told you to tell me. Well, I acted like you were some kind of idiot. But I want you to know that all three things were accurate and changed my life. My marriage has been restored, my spiritual life has been turned around, and now I am involved in leadership at a church. Thank you for taking the risk and stepping out to speak to me! I am very grateful." Well, I was blown away and realized that if we take the risk of doing "one act of obedience," it can change someone's life forever.

The key to Jesus' miracles was His obedience to the Father. In the Gospel of John, Jesus said that whatever He saw the Father doing, He did the same. In Paul's letter to the Philippians, 2:8, it tells us that Jesus humbled Himself by becoming obedient even to the point of death on the cross.

When you study the miracles Jesus did in the Gospels, you find that He didn't always do them the same way. On one occasion, He made mud and put it on the eyes of a man born blind and told him to go wash in the pool of Salome. When the man did, his eyes were healed, and he could see. On another occasion, Jesus put His fingers in a deaf and dumb man's ears and put spit on His tongue, told his ears to open and tongue to be loosed, and he was healed. On another occasion, he told a paralyzed man to take up his bed and walk. He told servants at a wedding feast to fill waterpots with water and take some to the wedding master, and when they did, the water became wine. Why was Jesus doing this? Because He was responding in obedience to the leading and voice of the Holy Spirit. Jesus isn't just our Savior; He is our example of how we are to live and act. The Apostle Paul told those he was discipling to follow him as he followed Christ. Jesus said in the Gospel of John, chapter 14, verse twelve, "He who believes in Me, the works that I do he will do also." How are we going to do the works that Jesus did? By following His example of obedience!

Now I know that what I just shared is bringing up all kinds of questions. Probably the number one question is, "How do you hear God's voice?" Allow me to share with you what I have learned about hearing God's voice.

First, I had to believe that I could hear God's voice. As I shared in chapter 1, hearing God's voice was what led me to Jesus. I believed it was normal for Christians to hear God's voice. Later as I read the Bible, I discovered that in the Gospel of John, chapter 10, Jesus said four times that His sheep would hear His voice. If you are one of His sheep, then you can hear His voice. If you believe that Jesus is your Savior and have been born again, to be transformed and made alive through faith in Jesus, then you are His sheep. The next thing I had to learn was that God speaks to us through different means and in different ways.

The primary way that God speaks to us is through His Word, the Bible. I have discovered that the more I read and meditate on the scriptures in the Bible, the more I hear God speak to me. How many times have you been reading the Bible, and suddenly, a passage of scripture just seems to jump off the page and is speaking directly to you? Well, guess what, that is God speaking to you.

"For the word of God is alive and powerful. It is sharper than the sharpest two-edged sword, cutting between soul and spirit, between joint and marrow. It exposes our

innermost thoughts and desires" (Hebrews 4:12, NLT). Did you notice that? The Word of God is alive. That means that it speaks to us now!

When I was pastoring my first church, it didn't go well. When I became the pastor, the church was one hundred people. Three years later, it had declined to sixty people. To say I was discouraged was an understatement! One day I was sitting in my living room feeling very depressed, and I decided to do a point and shoot in the Bible. I closed my eyes and let my Bible fall open in my lap and then put my finger down on the page. When I opened my eyes, I found my finger on the Gospel of John 10:10, "The thief comes only to steal and kill and destroy; I came that they may have life and have it abundantly." I thought, *I am doing really good on the steal, kill and destroy part. But if this is life and life more abundantly, God, You can have it!* Then the Lord began to speak to me and say, "You don't understand, Fred. It is not that you want to have life and life more abundantly; I died expecting you to have it."

Then the Lord began to remind me of many of the moves of God that had happened throughout history. Movements like the reformation, which began through Martin Luther, a Catholic priest, in the fourteenth century. He discovered that salvation was by grace through faith and not by becoming a member of the church. The Anabaptists in the sixteenth century believed that infant baptism was not a valid baptism, but that baptism was to take place after a salvation experience. In the 1700s, John and Charles Wesley discovered that there was a second work of grace called "the baptism of fire of the Holy Spirit." Because of it, they were used by the Lord to bring multitudes to salvation. Then there was an outpouring of the Holy Spirit at Azusa Street in Los Angeles in 1906, which reawakened the power of God and gifts of the Holy Spirit. He showed me that every one of these movements was for the purpose of restoring a truth that had been lost to the church.

Then the Lord said to me, "You have been a part of a move of God. The Jesus' People/Charismatic Movement." And I said, "Yes, Lord." Then He shocked me and said, "There has been another move, and you have missed it!" I said, "And what move would that be?" I was pretty sure that I was up to date and aware of any moves of God that were happening in the world. He said, "It is the Faith Movement!" I said, "The Faith Movement, those nuts?" The only people I had met from the Faith Movement were strange. He said, "No, this is Me, and if you don't get the truth I am revealing in this movement, you can't go on to the next one." I began to think about what I knew and understood about faith and discovered I knew very little. The fact is that everything that comes to us from God is by faith. Without it, we can't please God. For the next several years, I went on a quest to learn everything I could about faith. Everything in my church turned around as I put what I was learning into practice. Now, remember all this was triggered from one verse of Scripture. John 10:10: "The thief does not come except to steal, and to kill, and to destroy. I have come that they may have life, and that they may have *it* more abundantly." I don't know where you are now in your walk with Jesus but know this: He wants you to hear His voice speaking to you! Read on in the next chapter as I explain how God speaks to us!

Chapter Eight

HEARING GOD'S VOICE

Part Two

Another way the Lord speaks to us is through our emotions. We see someone hurting or looking defeated or cast down, and our heart goes out to them. Another way to say it is that we are moved with compassion. This was one of the main ways Jesus discerned the Father's voice. He would be moved with compassion and step out to meet the need. To hear God's voice this way, we must walk through life with our eyes open and really see the people we pass by. Most of us live in our own little self-centered bubble and are oblivious to the hurting people all around us every day.

One of the things I have been doing this past year is to do a four-mile walk around my neighborhood, praying and claiming my neighbors for God's kingdom. In doing this, I have had many opportunities to encounter my neighbors and represent the kingdom of God to them. The other day as I was walking, I saw a lady who was on crutches getting into her car in her garage. I thought I probably should talk to her. I decided to take another lap or two around the neighborhood, and if I saw her again, I would talk to her. A little while later, as I passed by her house, she had just got back and was about to go into her house through the door in her garage. I yelled out to her and said, "What's wrong with your leg?" She stopped and turned to look at me and said, "I have cancer." I walked a little closer, and she told me that this past year was the worst year of her life because both her parents had passed away, and her twenty-nine-year-old son had died as well. I began to talk to her about a God Who heals and cares about her. She said she had just started to learn more about the Bible from her brother-in-law, who was doing an online Bible study. She said that she had just gone to get a scan done on her leg because the doctors were concerned the cancer they operated on and removed had come back. I laid hands on her and commanded the cancer to leave her body. She said she was driving down to UCLA medical center in a few days to get the results of the scan. I ran into her on one of my walks a week later, and she told me the scan came back clear. Then she told me she was going to start going to church and has been going ever since.

Why did all this happen? Simply because I was moved by the Lord's compassion. Romans 5:5 tells us that the love of God has been poured out in our hearts by the Holy Spirit. God wants to pour His compassion through us to meet the needs of hurting people. God's love is already in us; we just need to allow it to flow through us. Lord, use us to be a manifestation of Your love.

Another way He speaks to us is by visions and dreams. On the day of Pentecost, the Apostle Peter quoted the prophet Joel, "'And it shall be in the last days,' God says, 'that I will pour out My Spirit on all mankind; and your sons and your daughters will prophesy, and your young men will see visions, and your old men will have dreams'" (Acts 2:17, NASB). I would have to say that over the last fifty years, I have experienced more visions than dreams. Maybe that means I'm not old yet.

One of the most dramatic visions I had, happened while I was on a twenty-one-day fast. It was the seventeenth day of the fast, and I was on my knees praying on the couch in my upstairs office in my house. It was the middle of the afternoon. I was praying from Ezekiel 37, Ezekiel's vision of the valley of dry bones. I was praying passionately over the church in America, concerned that we had become dead, dry bones. I was following Ezekiel's example of prophesying to the wind of the Holy Spirit to breathe on a dead church. While I was praying, I happened to look up and see, through the windows in my office, that the huge oak tree in my backyard was on fire. The flames were shooting up through the branches. I jumped to my feet and started to run out to go and get a hose to spray the tree.

Then I realized that it was not real. I was having what some Christians call an "open vision." While I watched the tree burning, the Holy Spirit spoke to me and said, "This is the fire of nuclear destruction!" My mind started racing with panic thoughts. I thought, *We have gone too far, and God is bringing judgment on America. How will I prepare my family and my church?* This was so real to me because just one mile from my house was a missile silo armed with an inter-ballistic missile aimed at some nation in the world. Then the Holy Spirit spoke again and said, "Or this is the fire of my Holy Spirit being poured out on America. Which one it is, He said, is up to you!" I knew that when He said you, He didn't mean me personally but the church in America. "If My people who are called by My name will humble themselves, and pray and seek My face, and turn from their wicked ways, then I will hear from heaven, and will forgive their sin and heal their land" (2 Chronicles 7:14). Out of this experience, I became a committed, praying Christian for our nation. I would recommend that you become one as well!

So, what does God's voice sound like? It sounds like our voice. In 1 Samuel 3, the boy Samuel was lying down to go to sleep when he heard a voice call out, "Samuel, Samuel." He got up and ran to the high priest, Eli, and said, "You called me." Eli told him he didn't call him and to go back to bed. As he laid down, he heard the voice again and ran to Eli again. Eli told him again that he didn't call him and to go back to bed. It happened a third time, and when Samuel went to Eli's room, Eli perceived that the Lord was speaking to him. He told Samuel that if he heard the voice again to say, "Speak, Lord, your servant is listening." Samuel did what Eli said, and the Lord told him about Eli's future.

What do we learn from this? First off, we learn that the Lord's voice sounds just like us. Secondly, we see that God's voice is something we learn to hear. Over time we become familiar with God's voice. Have you ever answered your phone and immediately knew who was calling you without looking at their caller ID? You knew who it was because you had become familiar with their voice. The same is true with hearing God's voice. Over time you begin to know when it is Him talking to you.

How can we be sure it is God speaking to us? Three ways.

One, does what you hear line up with what the Bible teaches? When God speaks to us, what He says will always line up with the teachings of the Bible. If what you are hearing is contrary to the Word of God, then you can rest assured it isn't God speaking

Two, does it challenge us to do something that requires faith on our part? Another way to spell faith is *risk*. In other words, it moves us out of our comfort zone and requires risk on our part. I have found that when God tells me to do something, it is something I can't do with my own strength or ability. I need God's grace which is His power working in my weakness, to do it. Romans 5:2 says that we enter into grace by faith. As I step out by faith to do what God is asking me, I receive the grace I need to do it.

Three, when we act on it, it produces fruit for God's kingdom. Does obeying what we hear God saying produce results that benefit the building and spreading of God's kingdom?

Another way that God speaks to us is by thoughts or impressions that come to our souls. Our soul is made up of our mind, will, and emotions. Many times, a thought will drop into my mind, something I was not even thinking about, like my story about the Texas businessman. The thought will sound like a specific direction to do something. Go tell this person such and such. Or buy this person's groceries. Or ask this person a question. Right at that point, one of three things happen. Number one, I immediately act on what I hear, or number two, I reject the thought saying no to it. Or number three, I reason my way out of responding to it, "That's really dumb," or "They really don't want to hear what I have to say," or "They will think I am an idiot or a religious nut, and that would be embarrassing."

When Saul of Tarsus was struck down by a light from heaven on the way to persecute Christians in Damascus, he heard Jesus say, "Why are you persecuting Me?" He was struck blind and ended up lying blind in a house on Straight Street for three days. While he was in this condition, there was a disciple named Ananias who lived nearby. Ananias heard God's voice tell him to go to the house and pray for Saul, who would become the great Apostle, Paul. At first, he began to reason with the Lord saying, "I heard about this man, Saul, and how much harm he has done to Christians in Jerusalem and that he has been given authority by the high priest to arrest those who call on Your name." The Lord answered him, telling him that Saul was a chosen vessel that He would greatly use. You can see that Ananias was trying to reason his way out of doing what he believed the Lord was saying because he was afraid. What if Ananias had given into his reasoning? He would have missed out on sowing into the life of probably the greatest apostle in history.

As you learn to hear God's voice, be quick to respond, and don't let reasoning keep you from the miracles He has planned for your life.

Chapter Nine

GOD WANTS YOUR BODY!

Several years ago, I had just finished ministering in Scotland and was taking a train from Edinburgh, Scotland, south to Peterborough, England. It was going to be a three-hour train ride. Well, at that time, I had learned to pray a prayer based on Romans 12:1, "I beseech you therefore, brethren, by the mercies of God, that you present your bodies a living sacrifice, holy, acceptable to God, *which is* your reasonable service." I would say, "Lord, today I make myself available to be used by You to be a witness for You today."

I went and boarded the train and got on the car that I was assigned to. I went with an expectation that there would be a divine appointment waiting for me on the train. As I climbed in and walked into my car, there were only three people in the car with me, a married couple and one other person. As I walked to my seat, I passed by the married couple, and I could hear the wife talking; she had an American accent.

As I passed by, I said, "You're from America," she said, "Yes, I am." I said, "What state?" She said, "California." I said, "I'm from California." She said, "What city?" I said, "San Jose." She said, "I'm from San Jose!" Then she said, "What high school did you go to?" I said, "Camden High School." She said, "I went to Camden High School!" Now, what are the odds that I would get on a train traveling from Scotland to a city in England, and there would be another person who not only lived in the same city I grew up in but went to the same high school? I immediately thought, *It's divine appointment time!*

She told me that her husband was from Scotland. Then she asked me what I was doing in Scotland. I told her that I was going around to churches, high schools, and colleges, telling people how to have a relationship with God. "Oh," she said, "that's nice." The whole time I spoke with her, her husband wouldn't even look up at me or acknowledge that I was even there. He just kept looking down in his lap.

Well, that was the end of our conversation, so I went and sat in my assigned seat. I thought, *Was that it, Lord? That was the whole divine appointment?* Well, I sat there for the whole three-hour trip and read a book. As we were coming into Peterborough, I got all my luggage together and hung it on both shoulders, and walked to the opening between the train cars where I would be getting off. Back then, when I traveled, I always carried too much luggage. I knew that I would only have a short time to get off the train when it stopped.

As I stood there, the train came to a stop a mile out from the station. A voice came on the loudspeaker announcing that there was a train broken down ahead of us at the station and we would be delayed for a short time. I thought, *Great!* So, I took all my bags off and set them down and just stood there waiting. Suddenly, I became aware that someone was standing really close to me. As I turned to look, here stood the lady from California's husband with his face just inches from mine. He had tears in his eyes and said to me, "Would you tell me how to have a relationship with God?" So, I shared my testimony with him and then led him to Jesus. As soon as we finished praying, the train jerked and pulled on into the station, and I got off. They stayed on the train, and I never saw them again.

I have had many other encounters just like that, and I believe that they were the result of me praying that simple prayer, "Lord, I make myself available to You to be used by You today." Prayer opens opportunities for obedience, and obedience connects God's power and presence to a miracle. So, let's take a closer look at Romans 12:1: "I beseech you therefore, brethren, by the mercies of God, that you present your bodies a living sacrifice, holy, acceptable to God, *which is* your reasonable service."

These words were written by the great Apostle, Paul. He starts out by saying, "I beseech you." I'm sure "beseech" is a word you haven't used lately or ever, for that matter. "Beseech" means to beg or plead or encourage passionately! Have you beseeched anyone lately?

Close your eyes and picture that the guest speaker at church this Sunday is the great Apostle, Paul. When he comes to the front to speak, he gets down on his knees and begins to beg us to do the next thing he is going to say. Would that get our attention? Well, that is what he is saying in this passage. Paul is begging, pleading, and passionately encouraging us to do what he is asking in this scripture.

Then he says, "By the mercies of God," which means, in lieu of all of God's mercies given to us through the death and resurrection of His Son, Jesus Christ, here is the least you can do for Him. Present your bodies as a living sacrifice. What does "a living sacrifice" mean?

I don't know about you, but when I was going to school, especially on the first day of school, the teachers would take a roll call. For me, it was the most dreaded day of the school year. Why? Because the teacher would start reading off each student's name out loud one by one, and we would have to respond, "Here" or "Present." The reason I dreaded it was because, inevitably, the teacher would mispronounce my last name in front of the whole class. I am convinced a demon made them do it. My last name is Kropp; it sounds like *crop*. But they would always pronounce it Krapp; it sounds like *crap*. Right there, I would die a thousand deaths as the entire class would laugh, knowing that would be their joke about me the rest of the year.

When I first read, "Present your body a living sacrifice," to me, it meant that every day God was taking a roll call to see who was present and available for He to use. At least I am sure He could pronounce my name right. Our response should be "Present" or "Available." The last phrase of Romans 12:1 is "Which is your reasonable service." So, I figured that the only reasonable thing for me to do was to make myself available to God the first thing every day!

Oh yeah, there is one more phrase, "Holy and acceptable to God." Don't let that phrase trip you up and make you feel unqualified for God to use you. You have been made holy by the blood of Jesus and have been accepted in the beloved. The Apostle Paul writes that God, "Having predestined us to adoption as sons by Jesus Christ to Himself, according to the good pleasure of His will, to the praise of the glory of His grace, by which He made us accepted in the Beloved" (Ephesians 1:5–6). In other words, through our faith in Jesus' sacrifice on the cross, we have right standing with God, the Father, and have been accepted as His children.

I believe that the Christian life is to be an adventure with God! Ephesians 2:10 says that we are God's masterpiece, created in Christ Jesus for good works, which God has prepared beforehand for us to walk in. Jesus said He came to give us life and life more abundantly (John 10:10). The Greek word for "abundantly" in the New Testament is *perisos*, which means superabundant in quantity, superior in quality to a normal, natural life! God doesn't want us to settle for a normal, natural life when we can live a supernatural life.

One of the main secrets to living the supernatural life

is to present your body daily to God, saying the words of Isaiah the prophet, "Here I am, send me!"

What if you and I and every born-again Christian on the planet got up every morning and prayed that prayer? Imagine the divine appointments and miracles that would happen. It would not only change us but would impact the eternal destiny of millions of lost people.

Why don't you stop reading right now and put this book down and present your body to the Lord!

Chapter Ten

GOD WROTE A BOOK ABOUT YOU!

We had been praying for three hours every Saturday night at one of our church member's homes for two and a half years. When we started the prayer meeting, our member's home was brand new. He had a large living room with a vaulted ceiling two stories high. The living room was so large the furniture was placed in the middle of it. There was a six-to-eight-foot space around the outside of the furniture. When you pray in the same room for over two years, everyone establishes their place of prayer in the room. My place was behind one of the couches. Every week I'd either pace back and forth behind the couch or lie on the floor behind it. I had paced there for so long that I had created a worn-out area in his brand-new carpet.

We began the prayer meeting each night with one focus, "Lord, teach us to pray." At the beginning of each meeting, I would say to the Lord, "We're going to stay in this room for three hours, so pray through us." Sometimes we would have amazing Holy Spirit-led and inspired prayer times, and other times, we would just be in the room for three hours. The number of people attending would fluctuate between eight and ten. It was Saturday night again, and here we were for another three-hour prayer meeting. This night turned out to be different than I had expected. I was in my normal place behind the couch and decided to lay face down on the carpet. I don't know how long I had been lying there, but I decided to get up.

When I tried to get up, I found that I couldn't lift my head up off the carpet. I thought to myself, *I don't remember being this tired when I came in.* Then I became aware that all my physical strength had gone out of my body. Then I realized that the presence of God had come upon me, and like others in the Bible who, when they encountered God's presence, lost all their physical strength. The next thing I knew, I was caught up out of my body and was standing between two rows of books in a library. As I looked at the books on the shelves in front of me, I saw that they were very old-looking books. Also, they were covered with a thick layer of dust.

Then the Holy Spirit said to me, "This is the library of heaven." (Later, after the experience, I thought, *Don't they have cleaning angels in heaven?* Just a little joke.) As I continued to look at the books, the Holy Spirit said, "Each one of these books represents my will for a city on the earth." Then I saw a hand go up in front of me and take one of the books off the shelf. The Holy Spirit said to me, "Because you have prayed these last two and a half years, now my will is going to be done in this city." Then the book fell open in the hand, and the scene changed, and it had become a poster nailed on a telephone pole. It had now become a proclamation. At first, I couldn't make out the words on the poster because they were out of focus. Then, I could read a few lines that said, "As Bethlehem was to Jerusalem, so this city will be to Kansas City."

Then I was instantly back in my body. I didn't say anything to the others in the room because I needed to research the Bible to make sure this experience was from the Lord. Is there a library in heaven? Are there books in heaven? Well, of course, I knew that there was at least one book, the Lamb's book of life. Those who have their names written in it will spend eternity with Jesus in heaven. Those who don't will spend eternity apart from God in a place called hell. As I searched the Scriptures, I saw that there were many books in heaven.

> *And I saw the dead, small and great, standing before God, and books were opened. And another book was opened, which is the Book of Life. And the dead were judged according to their works, by the things which were written in the books.*
>
> **Revelation 20:12**

Then I discovered that there is a book written by God about each one of us before we were ever born. I found it in Psalm 139:15–16:

My frame was not hidden from You, when I was made in secret, and skillfully wrought in the lower parts of the earth. Your eyes saw my substance, being yet unformed. And in Your book they all were written, the days fashioned for me, when as yet there were none of them.

Psalm 139:15–16

In that book is God's perfect will and plan for our lives. But I learned from my encounter in heaven's library that God's plan and will for us would not automatically happen. We must pray until God's plans for us are released from heaven to earth. This is why Jesus said, "When you pray, say, Your kingdom come Your will be done on earth as it is in heaven." Your book is in heaven, but you must pray it into your life here on earth. I heard Dr. David Yonggi Cho, the pastor of the largest church in the world in Korea, say one time, "You are walking on the prayers you prayed six months ago."

How many of you have ever read or heard Jeremiah 29:11? *"For I know the thoughts that I think toward you, says the LORD, thoughts of peace and not of evil, (the New International Version says to prosper you and not to harm you) to give you a future and a hope."* We all like that verse, but we fail to read the next few verses that explain how God's plan to prosper us is going to happen. *"Then you will call upon me and come and pray to me, and I will hear you. You will seek me and find me, when you seek me with all your heart. I will be found by you, declares the LORD, and I will restore your fortunes"*

(Jeremiah 29:12–14, ESV).

Persistent, consistent prayer is what opens the book the Lord has written about you and releases His plan and destiny in your life. We see this in the life of Daniel, the prophet. In Daniel, chapter 10, Daniel is praying and fasting for three weeks concerning a revelation the Lord had given him about Israel's return from captivity. At the end of the three weeks, the angel Gabriel came to him to tell him that God had heard his prayer from the very beginning of his fast. He came to let Daniel know that God was answering his prayer and that the evil forces of the devil had been resisting the breakthrough from happening. Ephesians 6:12 tells us that we are wrestling with principalities and rulers of darkness in the heavenly places. These are fallen angels who control countries, regions, and places. Ephesians 6:18 tells us to pray at all times in the Spirit, be alert with all perseverance, and petition for the saints.

Let me share another experience I had during that two-and-a-half-year prayer meeting. One night somewhere in the middle of the three hours. I began to pray, "Strengthen the battle, strengthen the battle, strengthen the battle over and over again." Pretty soon, everyone in the room was saying the same thing. Suddenly, I heard a noise in the atmosphere above the house. It was the sound of clanging swords and heavy breathing. It was the sound of two armies of angels fighting each other. It was God's angels and the devil's angels in battle. I could tell that our saying, "Strengthen the battle," over and over, was giving strength to God's angels, and they were defeating the enemy and pushing them back. Then I heard the devil's angels start to drop their swords and armor and run. I don't think anyone else in the room was hearing this but me, but we were all engaged in the unified declaration.

Then I saw a vision of myself kneeling before God's throne, and an angel was putting a red cape on me. I said to the Lord, "What does this mean?" and He answered me, "Nahum chapter 2." I thought, *What? I hardly remembered that Nahum was a book in the Bible.* I apologize to all of you that have memorized the books of the Bible. I opened Nahum, chapter 2, and read these words,

> *The one who scatters has come up against you. Keep watch over the fortress, watch the road; Bind up your waist, summon all your strength. The shields of his warriors are dyed red, the warriors are dressed in scarlet, the chariots are fitted with flashing steel when he is prepared to march, and the juniper spears are brandished. The chariots drive wildly in the streets, they rush around in the public squares; their appearance is like torches, they drive back and forth like lightning flashes.*
>
> **Nahum 2:1, 3–4 (NASB)**

It sounds like a battle is going on in this scripture. God was confirming to me that there really was a spiritual battle going on that night, and somehow, we were taking part in it through our prayer declarations. Then I noticed the phrase, "The warriors are dressed in scarlet." That's what the red cape the angel was putting on me was. Somehow,

I had gained a position of authority in the spiritual realm because we had been praying consistently for two and a half years. I remembered that God sent an angel to a Roman Centurion in Acts 10 to tell him that his prayers and alms had become a memorial before God in heaven.

It reminds me of when the seven sons of Sceva in Acts 19:14 were trying to cast out demons in the name of Jesus, who Paul preached. The demon said to them, "Jesus, I know, and Paul, I know, but who are you?" The demonized man went on to beat them up and strip them naked and run them out of the house. It doesn't matter if everybody in the world knows your name. What matters is that God and the devils' demonic forces know who you are. When you pray consistently and persistently, you get both heaven's and hell's attention. The enemy wants to hold back your destiny and keep you from experiencing the things God has written in your book! Persistent, consistent prayer will open the book in your life.

This is why when one of the disciples asked Jesus, "Lord, teach us to pray." He answered, "When you pray, say, 'Your kingdom come, Your will be done on earth as it is in heaven.'"

My prayer for you is that you experience everything that God has written in His book about you!

Chapter Eleven

I CHOOSE YOU!

When I was a kid growing up, I wasn't great at sports. I always dreaded the times when the PE teacher would say, "Line up, we're going to choose teams. Mike and John, you are the team captains, so start choosing your team members." (Maybe you have had this experience.) Mike and John would take turns calling out names for their teams. Inevitably they would choose all the good players until they got down to the last two, which would be me and some other uncoordinated kid, let's say his name was Eddie. Mike would say something like, "John, you take Eddie, and I guess I'm stuck with Fred." It didn't always happen that way; sometimes, I was second to last. This contributed to my belief that I was a reject and that no one wanted to choose me. This played out through my high school and college-age years in many of my relationships, deepening the belief that no one wanted me.

As my friend Carmelo, who came from a gang background and is now an amazing man of God, would say, "But Jesus!" Then, at twenty-two years of age, on the side of a mountain in Lake Tahoe, Nevada, God reached down from heaven and, without words, said, "I choose you!"

Maybe you have felt the same way about yourself. Well, I have good news for you, you're in good company. A boy named David, who was the son of Jesse, and the youngest of eight brothers, who later became the great King David, had the same experience.

Because God had rejected the current king, Saul, because of his disobedience, he sent the Prophet Samuel to the house of Jesse to anoint the next king of Israel. When Samuel arrived at Jesse's house, he began to look at Jesse's sons. When Samuel looked at Eliab, Jesse's oldest, he was handsome and tall, and Samuel thought, "For sure, this is the Lord's anointed standing before him!" Then the Lord spoke these words to Samuel.

> *But the LORD said to Samuel, 'Do not look on his appearance or on the height of his stature, because I have rejected him. For the LORD sees not as man sees, man looks on the outward appearance, but the LORD looks on the heart.'*
>
> **1 Samuel 16:7 (ESV)**

Jesse then brought six of his other sons before Samuel, and Samuel told Jesse that the Lord did not choose any of them. Then Samuel asked Jesse if he had any other sons.

Jesse told Samuel that there was just his youngest son David who was out watching over the sheep. Samuel said, "Send for him because we are not going to eat until you bring him here." I would imagine the brothers made haste in bringing David in, knowing they were not going to eat until he was there.

When David arrived, the Lord told Samuel to anoint him, saying, "This is him!" When Samuel anointed David, the Spirit of God came upon David mightily!

Now let's take a closer look at this. Jesse, David's father, and David's brothers believed that David was so insignificant and unimportant that they didn't even bother to bring him into the house with the others. Later, when David went to bring food to his brothers who were in battle formation against the Philistine army, Eliab put David down, rebuking him for even being there. So, just because people don't choose you doesn't mean that you are not chosen.

Allow me to prove to you the fact that God chooses you!

God has chosen us in Christ! The Apostle Paul writes, "Even as he (God) chose us in him (Jesus) before the foundation of the world, that we should be holy and blameless before him. In love" (Ephesians 1:4, ESV). Paul says it again in his letter to the church at Thessalonica. "We should always give thanks to God for you, brothers *and sisters* beloved by the Lord, because God has chosen you from the beginning for salvation through sanctification by the Spirit and faith in the truth" (2 Thessalonians 2:13, NASB).

99

Jesus, Himself has chosen us. Jesus said, "You did not choose Me, but I chose you, and appointed you that you would go and bear fruit, and *that* your fruit would remain, so that whatever you ask of the Father in My name He may give to you" (John 15:16, NASB).

God chooses the people who everyone else rejects. The Apostle Paul writes,

> *For consider your calling, brothers and sisters, that there were not many wise according to the flesh, not many mighty, not many noble; but God has chosen the foolish things of the world to shame the wise, and God has chosen the weak things of the world to shame the things which are strong, and the insignificant things of the world and the despised God has chosen, the things that are not, so that He may nullify the things that are, so that no human may boast before God.*
>
> **1 Corinthians 1:26–29 (NASB)**

God chooses you so you can shine for Him and be a trophy of His unmerited favor and grace. "But you *are* a chosen generation, a royal priesthood, a holy nation, His own special people, that you may proclaim the praises of Him who called you out of darkness into His marvelous light" (1 Peter 2:9).

So, let's settle it once and for all! You are one of God's chosen ones! You are on God's team! You are in God's family! It wasn't because you were the best, the brightest, the strongest, the best looking, or any other reason someone might be chosen. He chose you because

He loved you, and He made a way for you to be chosen. He saw that you would respond to the Gospel and say yes to Jesus. The moment you believed in Jesus' death and resurrection. The moment you understood that He paid the price for your sin. At that moment that you were born again and became one of God's chosen!

He chose you because He looked at your heart and saw the potential of Christ in you! He saw Jesus being exalted through your weakness, lack of skills, and talent. Just look at the disciples Jesus chose. Most were uneducated, self-centered, and full of fear and doubt. They argued about who was going to be the greatest. They wanted to know what was in it for them. Tax collectors were some of the people the Jews hated the most. Matthew was a tax collector. How about Saul, who became the great Apostle, Paul? He was on the way to persecute and arrest Christians, and the Lord looked down from heaven and said, "I choose him!"

Well, you say, "I have failed God too many times, so how could He still choose me?" Well, He does! He still chooses you. So, get back up, dust yourself off, and get in the game. He is still for you and has things for you to do that He planned before the foundation of the world! "For the gifts and the calling of God *are* irrevocable" (Romans 11:29).

Take a moment right now to acknowledge that you have been chosen by the Lord to do exploits for His glory! Remember, you didn't choose Him, but He chose you to bear much fruit!

Chapter Twelve

CHRIST IN YOU

When I was young, I remember when my family purchased our first new car. It was a 1954 Chevrolet Belair four-door with a power glide automatic transmission. It was yellow with a green top and had a new special feature, genuine vinyl seats that were also yellow and green. (Back then, vinyl was popular, and only the rich could afford genuine leather.) My mother, who was an Italian Catholic, especially liked the car. The reason she did was that it had a solid steel dashboard, not like today, where we have padded dashboards, seatbelts, and airbags. If we got in a wreck, we completely smashed ourselves on it. The reason she loved the steel dashboard was that she could put a little plastic statue of Jesus on it, and He would stay right there because He had a magnet on the bottom. The Catholics believed that the plastic Jesus would protect them from accidents and harm. Not too long after we bought the car, we got in an accident while my mom was driving at night. She went off the road because of the fog and hit a tree. My brother and I were asleep in the back seat, and I remember being thrown off onto the floor. Well, we all survived, and no one was injured. So, our plastic Jesus saved us!

Years later, after I had become a Christian, I read the verse in Colossians 1:27: *"To them God willed to make known what are the riches of the glory of this mystery among the Gentiles: which is Christ in you, the hope of glory."*

It meant that Jesus Christ, the Son of God, comes to live inside of those who are born again. I remembered that the Sunday school teachers would ask the little kids, "Where is Jesus?" and they would point to their chest and say, "In my heart." I began to ask the question, "How big is the Jesus that lives in us?" Then it hit me that the Catholics had more faith in their plastic Jesus on the dashboard of their car than the born-again Christians who have Jesus living inside of them. (I'm not saying that there are no born-again Catholics.)

Let's first establish from Scripture that God actually lives in us.

> Jesus declares He and the Father will come into those who open the door of their hearts to Him: *"Behold, I stand at the door and knock. If anyone hears My voice and opens the door, I will come in to him and dine with him, and he with Me"* (Revelation 3:20).
>
> *"At that day you will know that I am in My*

Father, and you in Me, and I in you" (John 14:20).

"Jesus answered and said to him, 'If anyone loves Me, he will keep My word; and My Father will love him, and We will come to him and make Our home with him'" (John 14:23).

"I in them, and You in Me; that they may be made perfect in one, and that the world may know that You have sent Me, and have loved them as You have loved Me" (John 17:23).

The Apostle Paul declares that we have been crucified with Christ and that Christ now lives in us: "I have been crucified with Christ; it is no longer I who live, but Christ lives in me; and the life which I now live in the flesh I live by faith in the Son of God, who loved me and gave Himself for me" (Galatians 2:20).

But you are not in the flesh but in the Spirit, if indeed the Spirit of God dwells in you. Now if anyone does not have the Spirit of Christ, he is not His. And if Christ is in you, the body is dead because of sin, but the Spirit is life because of righteousness.

Romans 8:9–10

We are the temple of the Living God:

And what agreement has the temple of God with idols? For you are the temple of the

*Living God. As God has said: 'I will dwell
in them and walk among them. I will be their
God, and they shall be My people.'*

2 Corinthians 6:16

Or do you not know that your body is the
temple of the Holy Spirit *who is* in you,
whom you have from God, and you are not
your own? For you were bought at a price;
therefore, glorify God in your body and in
your spirit, which are God's.

1 Corinthians 6:19–20

The Holy Spirit dwells in us and gives life to our mortal
bodies:

*"But if the Spirit of Him who raised Jesus
from the dead dwells in you, He who raised
Christ from the dead will also give life to your
mortal bodies through His Spirit who dwells
in you" (Romans 8:11).*

*And I will pray the Father, and He will give
you another Helper, that He may abide with
you forever—the Spirit of truth, whom the
world cannot receive, because it neither sees
Him nor knows Him; but you know Him, for
He dwells with you and will be in you.*

John 14:16–17

God is at work in us to will and work for His good
pleasure:

*"For it is God who works in you both to will and
to do for His good pleasure" (Philippians 2:13).*

106

We have God's power in us to do His work:

> *"To this end I also labor, striving according to His working which works in me mightily"* (Colossians 1:29).

> *"But we have this treasure in earthen vessels, that the excellence of the power may be of God and not of us"* (2 Corinthians 4:7).

> *"Now to Him who is able to do exceedingly abundantly above all that we ask or think, according to the power that works in us"* (Ephesians 3:20).

The Greater One lives in us:

> *"You are of God, little children, and have overcome them, because He who is in you is greater than he who is in the world"* (1 John 4:4).

I think that I have given you enough scriptural evidence to establish the fact that Jesus lives in you! Now let's answer the question, "How big is the Jesus Who lives inside of us?"

Years back, I was listening to some scientists discussing how big the universe was on the radio. They said that they still haven't found the end of it but that they guessed it was at least ten billion light-years big. Well, a light-year is how far light travels in a year. Light travels 670,616,629,000 miles in one hour. Three hundred and sixty-five days in a year has 8,760 hours in it. So light travels 5,878,499,817,000 miles in a single year. (Yep, that is almost six trillion miles.) So if you multiply 5,878,499,817,000 by 10 billion light-years, it is 5,878, 499,817,000,000,000,000,000,000,000,000 miles. Whew, that makes me dizzy! I don't even know what to call that number, but the scientists say that the universe is at least that big.

Now how many of you believe that God created the universe? Here is an interesting Bible fact, Isaiah the Prophet tells us that God measured out the universe with a span in Isaiah 46:12. A "span" is the distance between your thumb and your little finger, about six or seven inches. So, when God was deciding how big to make the universe, He stretched out His hand and said, "I will make it that big!" Can someone please say, "Big God"?

I don't know about you, but I need to get a much bigger revelation of how big the Jesus who lives inside of me really is! And then the Apostle Paul says, "I can do all things through Christ who strengthens me." Jesus said in the Gospel of John 14:12, "Those who believe in me, the works that I do shall they do also." That begins to make more sense when you understand how big the Jesus inside of you really is. This really becomes powerful when the Apostle John says, "He who is in you is greater than He who is in the world." Speaking of the devil, Satan, Lucifer, come on, somebody, let's say, "Big God, little devil!"

It's time for you to release the reality of Christ in you through your life and experience the supernatural power of God working mightily in you!

Chapter Thirteen

KEYS TO COURAGE

If we are going to walk in acts of obedience, it is going to take something called "courage"!

The dictionary defines "courage" as "the mental or moral strength to venture, persevere, and withstand danger, fear, or difficulty. The attitude of facing and dealing with anything recognized as dangerous, difficult, or painful instead of withdrawing from it. The quality of being fearless or brave; valor. The bravery and/or strength to do something that could be dangerous. The ability to do things which one finds frightening."

Many years ago, Pam and I were involved in a halfway house ministry where we took people off the streets for the purpose of deliverance and discipleship. At one point, we had a young man move in who was in his twenties. From all outward appearance, he seemed like a very nice and polite young man. One night we were sitting in the main living room when something triggered him, and he became instantly violent, pulling out a knife and threatening to stab someone. The next thing I knew, I ran over to him, grabbing him and pushing him against the wall, and held him there until he calmed down. After it was all over, I realized what a scary thing I had done.

Being courageous was not an attribute that I would describe as one of mine. When I was younger, I worked in construction as an apprentice. One day, we were working on the outside of a two-story house. We were on the second story, and my journeyman told me to bring a seventy-five-pound roll of chicken wire out to him on the scaffolding made up of two planks. Chicken wire is the wire they nail on the outside of a house that is going to be plastered with stucco. I know it was only two stories high, but heights weren't my thing. The thought of getting out and standing on those two flimsy planks terrorized me. So, I pushed the roll of chicken wire out onto the planks and crawled out on them pushing it along the planks. When my journeyman saw me, he yelled, saying, "What are you doing? Stand up!" That pretty much describes the level of my courage. Maybe courage and taking risks isn't one of your strengths either. If so, how are we going to do acts of obedience? So, what made me do this courageous act of disarming the young man? That is what this chapter is about!

The First Key to Courage

You need to understand that if stepping out to do acts of obedience is a challenge for you, you are in good company. Evidently, courage was going to be a problem for Joshua in the Bible. His assignment was, "Take the promised land by driving out and destroying the people living there, which included giants." The Lord had to tell Joshua over and over to be strong and courageous: "Be strong and of good courage, for to this people you shall divide as an inheritance the land which I swore to their fathers to give them" (Joshua 1:6).

> *Only be strong and very courageous, that you may observe to do according to all the law which Moses My servant commanded you; do not turn from it to the right hand or to the left, that you may prosper wherever you go.*
>
> **Joshua 1:7**

> *"Have I not commanded you? Be strong and of good courage; do not be afraid, nor be dismayed, for the LORD your God is with you wherever you go" (Joshua 1:9).*

> *"Now the LORD said to Joshua: 'Do not be afraid, nor be dismayed; take all the people of war with you, and arise, go up to Ai. See, I have given into your hand the king of Ai, his people, his city, and his land'" (Joshua 8:1).*

Why did the Lord say this to Joshua over and over? Because He knew fear was an issue for him!

How about Gideon? He was so afraid of the Midianites that he was beating out the wheat in a winepress so they wouldn't see him. Then an angel appears to him and calls him a mighty man of valor and that God is going to use him to lead the Israelites to defeat the Midianites. Before he was willing to go and do what God was asking him to do, he wanted a sign from heaven to prove this really was God. He put out a sheepskin two nights in a row. The first night Gideon asked God to make the sheepskin wet and all the ground around it dry, and God did it. The next night he asked that the opposite would happen, and God did it. Even with those two signs, Gideon still wasn't satisfied. God sent him down to the camp of the enemy to hear one of them tell a dream about a loaf of barley that rolled into the camp, destroying one of the tents. Another man who was with him interpreted the dream as it being none other than the sword of Gideon defeating the Midianites.

Fast forward to the New Testament. How about Jesus' main man, Peter? The bravest of Jesus' disciples! The one who wasn't afraid to get out of the boat and walk on water. The one who said, "Even if everyone forsakes You, I will never forsake You." The one who cut off the ear of the man who came into the crowd with Judas to arrest Jesus. Yes, that same Peter who denied he knew Jesus three times because of fear. Or, for that matter, how about all the other disciples who went into hiding after Jesus' arrest and crucifixion?

But something happened that turned these cowards into those who were willing to suffer and die for the Gospel. It was Pentecost, the day they were all filled with the Holy Spirit and fire! So, the first key to courage is for us to be filled with the Holy Spirit. Jesus said, "You shall receive power when the Holy Spirit has come upon you;

and you shall be witnesses to Me" (Acts 1:8). That is what triggered my courageous response in the face of danger. It was the Holy Spirit working in me.

The Second Key to Courage

The second key to courage is the love of God. "There is no fear in love; but perfect love casts out fear" (1 John 4:18). The more we are filled with God's love, the more courageous we will be. God so loved the world that He gave his only begotten Son so that those who believe in Him would not perish but have eternal life. As we are filled with greater measures of the love of God, we, too, will be willing to give our lives for the sake of others hearing the good news of Jesus. Jesus said, "Greater love has no one than this, than to lay down one's life for his friends" (John 15:13). Why would someone lay down their life for their friends? Because of the love he or she has for them.

The Third Key to Courage

The third key to courage is righteousness. "The wicked flee when no one pursues, but the righteous are bold as a lion" (Proverbs 28:1). According to this passage, righteousness produces boldness. Righteous people are passionate about justice and standing up for truth. They won't tolerate injustice and corruption without making a stand and doing something about it. What is going to turn America back to God? Righteous people who aren't ashamed of the Gospel and are willing to stand up against evil and speak the truth in love.

I know that what I am about to say will offend some. One of the reasons many Christians don't share the Gospel is because of unrighteousness. When we tolerate some area of sin in our lives, it diminishes our confidence and boldness. We fall into the trap of subconsciously thinking, *If the Gospel isn't working for me, why would I share it with others?* The good news is that Jesus became sin for us that we might become the righteousness of God in Him (2 Corinthians 5:21). If we confess and forsake our sins, He cleanses us from all unrighteousness.

The Fourth Key to Courage

The fourth key to courage is living our lives from an eternal perspective. (I write more about this in chapter 15.) Most Christians in America today live from a "temporal perspective" rather than an "eternal perspective." What does it mean to live from a temporal perspective? It means we only look at our lives in the here and now or in the time span of our lives in the sixty, seventy, or eighty years plus we live on the earth. We process our Christian life with the thoughts, *Am I blessed now? Am I healthy now? Am I safe now? Am I okay now? Am I happy now?* Because of this, we don't think eternally about our lives other than we want to go to heaven and not hell when we die. To live our lives from an eternal perspective is to view our lives in the light of eternity rather than just the here and now. We understand that life here is only temporary, and we are going to live forever in the afterlife. The last time I checked, eternity is a whole lot longer than seventy to ninety years on this planet. The problem with the temporal perspective is that it produces a self-centered, self-focused, self-preservation kind of life that leads to fear and ultimate disappointment.

Living life from an eternal perspective changes everything! It changes the value and importance of everything we do here and now. It brings into play eternal rewards and eternal losses. It asks one question for all people on the planet, "What is your eternal destination, and how will you spend eternity?" It now becomes the reason why sharing the Gospel is so vitally important. It also makes what we go through in this life insignificant compared to the glories and rewards that await us for all eternity. For us who are eternally minded, we are not of this world! This life isn't the end game for us! We are strangers and aliens from another kingdom that will last forever! We are only visiting this planet; it is not our home! We are looking for a city whose builder and maker is the Lord of lords and the King of kings! We are running the race set before us, enduring the tests and trials, knowing there are rewards awaiting us in heaven. Living from an eternal perspective sets us free from the self-centered, self-focused, self-preservation kind of life and causes us to live our lives for Jesus and His love for the lost and dying.

The Fifth Key to Courage

The fifth key to courage is to walk by faith and not by sight.

> *And what more shall I say? For the time would fail me to tell of Gideon and Barak and Samson and Jephthah, also of David and Samuel and the prophets: who through faith subdued kingdoms, worked righteousness, obtained promises, stopped the mouths of lions, quenched the violence of fire, escaped the edge of the sword, out of weakness were made strong, became valiant in battle, turned to flight the armies of the aliens.*
>
> **Hebrews 11:32–34**

Did you notice that it says that through faith, they became *valiant* in battle? Valiant means fearless, brave, heroic, bold, and yes, courageous! So, if faith makes us bold and courageous, how does it do that?

"Therefore, having been justified by faith, we have peace with God through our Lord Jesus Christ, through whom also we have access by faith into this grace in which we stand" (Romans 5:1–2). Notice that we have access by faith into grace. What does accessing grace have to do with courage? Well, grace is the desire, the power, and the ability to do the will of God. Grace is God's supernatural ability working through our weaknesses. The Apostle Paul writes,

But he (The Lord) said to me, 'My grace is sufficient for you, for my power is made perfect in weakness.' Therefore, I will boast all the more gladly of my weaknesses, so that the power of Christ may rest upon me.

2 Corinthians 12:9 (ESV)

Allow me to illustrate how this works. Let's say you are in a store and you see someone who is obviously sick. Maybe they are wearing a leg brace. You feel that the Lord wants you to go and pray for them, but just one problem. It seems too scary or embarrassing for you to do it. Now, I want you to close your eyes and imagine that there is a line on the floor in front of you. On this side of the line are your natural fears and hesitations. On the other side of the line are boldness and courage. To access grace to do what you believe the Lord is asking you to do, you must step across the line. Faith is stepping across the line. When you do, you will find God's power activated in your weakness, and the fears and intimidations will fall away! You will find yourself operating in a boldness you did not have one moment ago.

Again, to live lives that are courageous, we must be 1. continually filled with the Holy Spirit; 2. immersed in the love of God; 3. clothed with His righteousness; 4. living our life from an eternal perspective, and 5. accessing His grace by faith.

Chapter Fourteen

PROPHETIC ACTS OF OBEDIENCE

Years ago, I made several ministry trips to England. I would go for two weeks or a month at a time. During those trips, I ministered in churches, colleges, and high schools. There were times when I saw the Holy Spirit come upon whole congregations and groups with many types of Holy Spirit manifestations. For some, it was weeping, others uncontrolled laughter, others violent shaking, others cried out "I repent," and others falling to the floor. There was a church in Ely, England, which is near Cambridge, that would pre-arrange my speaking schedule.

On one of my trips, I was going to be going to several cities all over England. Prior to the trip, I organized a weekly prayer meeting with several of my church members on Tuesday nights five weeks prior to leaving. In preparation for the prayer meetings, I would make a list of all the churches and groups I would be speaking at. I would also make a map of England with all the locations shown and lines going between them showing the route I would be taking.

The purpose of the prayer meetings was to pray over each church or group and get the Lord's strategy for each one. The way we would do it is that I would break the prayer group up into groups of three giving each one the list and the map with the locations. Then I would have them pray for thirty minutes over them, writing down any words, pictures, or insights they would get while praying. Then we would come together, and I would have them share what the Lord was showing them. What they shared became the focus of our prayers.

One night I was in my group of three and was kneeling staring at the map. There was one area in the Southeast corner of England where the lines showing my travel itinerary formed a triangle. While I looked at the map, I felt the Lord say, "I have an assignment for you in the middle of the triangle." When I looked in the middle, there was a city called Canterbury. I must expose my ignorance as I didn't know the significance of Canterbury, which I will show later. When the groups of three came back together that night and began to share, one of them said that there was a principality, a ruling evil spirit that controls an institution, region, or a nation, that the Lord was going to use us to overthrow. Another one of the groups said the Lord had shown them it was a spirit of religion. Then I said, "I think I know where it is; it is in Canterbury."

The next day I had my secretary do research on

Canterbury. When she shared her findings with me, it shook me. She told me that there was a cathedral in Canterbury that was the center for the Church of England, like the Vatican in Rome for the Roman Catholic Church. From this, I concluded that sometime during the trip, I was to gather a group of intercessors and go to the cathedral there and bind a spirit of religion. My plan was to go to all the other places I was going to be ministering first and invite intercessors to join my wife, Pam, and me there on a Thursday afternoon at the end of the trip.

Well, the day finally arrived, and we had made our way to Canterbury, one of the most beautiful cities in England. Several intercessors from all over England joined us. There was a thick cloud hovering over the city that day as we gathered outside of the cathedral. There were benches we could sit on. As the group sat there, I began to preach a message about why we were there and the power of our prayers. As I spoke, a hole opened up in the clouds over us, and a ray of sunlight came down on us. As I was finishing my message, a young English man in his twenties, who had come to be with us, said, "Do you realize what is happening in the Church of England right now?" I said, "No."

He told us that they were about to select a new archbishop over the church. He said that the two main decision-makers who would select the next archbishop from a list of qualified candidates given to them by the bishops of the church were the Queen and the prime minister. He went on to tell us that the current archbishop was holding worship gatherings in the church's cathedral of people from all religions and even witches. He was claiming that they were all one and promoting unity together.

After this, I had the group walk around the outside of the cathedral seven times to bind the spirit of religion over the Church of England. Pam and I then made our way into the cathedral to walk around the inside and pray. Soon after we went inside, there was an announcement over the loudspeakers that everyone was to stop and remain silent. Then they prayed the Lord's prayer over the loudspeakers. This was a major sign of confirmation to us. I had been traveling for the last two and a half years in cities all over the US with a pastor named Larry Lea, teaching a seminar called "Could You Not Tarry One Hour." The seminar's purpose was to teach Christians how to pray for one hour a day using the Lord's Prayer as a guide.

Two months later, we were at home in the USA, and we received a copy of Charisma Magazine in the mail. As I scanned through it, my eyes landed on an article titled, "Church of England selects new archbishop." The article said that the new archbishop was a spirit-filled, charismatic Christian. And here was the shocker. He was not even on the list of names given to the Queen and prime minister, but by some miraculous work of God, he was chosen. Can somebody say, "Wow!"

Now, I am sure there were other Christians in England praying about who would be selected, but I know that the Lord sent us to be a part of making sure that His choice would happen and the spirit of religion would not have its way.

What can we learn from my experience?

First, we can learn that God has strategic works or prophetic acts that He has planned for each one of us. We can see this truth in Paul's letter to the church in Ephesus, "For we are his workmanship, created in Christ Jesus for good works, which God prepared beforehand, that we should walk in them" (Ephesians 2:10). God has predestined you and me to accomplish specific works that release God's will on earth.

Second, we can identify and activate those works by strategizing in prayer with other believers. What is strategizing in prayer? It is where we gather with other believers to pray about a certain topic or issue. While praying, we get the mind of the Lord and clear direction about it. You can see this in the Book of Acts, chapter 13.

> *Now there were prophets and teachers at Antioch, in the church that was there: Barnabas, Simeon who was called Niger, Lucius of Cyrene, Manaen who had been brought up with Herod the tetrarch, and Saul. While they were serving the Lord and fasting, the Holy Spirit said, 'Set Barnabas and Saul apart for Me for the work to which I have called them.' Then, when they had fasted, prayed, and laid their hands on them, they sent them away. So, being sent out by the Holy Spirit, they went down to Seleucia and from there they sailed to Cyprus.*

> **Acts 13:1–4 (NASB)**

Notice a group of leaders from the church at Antioch gave themselves to a protracted time of fasting, prayer, and worship to seek direction from the Lord. While they were doing this, they got directions from the Holy Spirit for specific people to follow. Then they acted in that direction. Now it doesn't tell us specifically how they heard the Holy Spirit speak to them. I'd like to think that they all got a revelation about certain parts of what the Lord wanted them to do, and when they shared their part with the whole group, the picture became clear. Now this passage in Paul's letter to the church at Corinth will make sense.

> *What then, brethren, is [the right course]? When you meet together, each one has a hymn, a teaching, a disclosure of special knowledge or information, an utterance in a [strange] tongue, or an interpretation of it. [But] let everything be constructive and edifying and for the good of all.*
> **1 Corinthians 14:26 (AMPC)**

Are you getting the picture? God reveals His will through the body of Christ as we come together to seek His direction.

The third thing we can learn from my experience is that when we do the one act of obedience, it releases the supernatural hand of God and causes His will to be done on earth as in heaven. We may or may not always see the results ourselves but know this: God is working through us to accomplish His purposes. It reminds me of an old chorus we used to sing, "Trust and obey, for there is no other way, to be happy in Jesus, but to trust and obey." The Lord has some prophetic acts of obedience for you to accomplish, pray right now that you won't miss any of them! This is a great adventure!

Chapter Fifteen

LIVING LIFE FROM A HEAVENLY ETERNAL PERSPECTIVE

"Perspective:" How something is viewed; the angle at which something is seen; a mindset toward life; how you visualize life, people, circumstances, ideologies, your purpose, yourself, and the way you view the world.

I was on a flight from Amsterdam, Holland, to New York. I had no sooner settled into my economy class seat when a stewardess came and asked me if I wouldn't mind moving up to business class because they needed my seat for another passenger. I didn't have to pray about it and immediately said, "I would be happy to." One of the things I have learned is that when there is a change in schedule, situation, or circumstance, there is more than likely a divine appointment being set up by the Holy Spirit. When I got to my new seat, there was no one seated next to me.

Then a young man came down the aisle who had camera equipment hanging all over him. I was seated on the aisle, and his seat was a window seat. He said with a kind of gruff voice, "That's my seat!" He started piling his equipment right over me into the seat without even giving me a chance to get up and get out of his way. Once he got situated, I asked why he was going to New York. He told me he was a photographer for Playboy magazine and that he had just done a playmate shoot in Amsterdam. I thought, *I've got one!* Then, he asked me what I did. I told him that I was a pastor and was coming back from a ministry trip in Europe. He looked at me angrily and said, "Don't you try to convert me!" I assured him that I wouldn't. End of conversation!

At that time, I carried a large leather-bound Bible with me. I got it out of my bag in the overhead compartment and placed it in my lap, and sat there smiling. Soon after we took off, he turned to me and said, "What does the Bible say about such and such? (I don't remember the exact question.) I looked at him and said, "Now, I'm not trying to convert you, right?" He said something like, "Yeah, no problem." So, I began to show him scriptures that spoke about his question. As soon as I finished, he asked me another question about what the Bible said on another topic. The flight to New York was six to seven hours, and that's how long we did a Bible study. By the end of the flight, he wasn't ready to accept Jesus yet, but that was the longest one on one Bible study I have ever done. The Apostle Paul said, "One plants and another waters, but God gives the increase." Jesus said that the seed that produces a harvest is the Word of God. I planted a lot of seeds in that young man on that flight.

What would motivate me to look for and act on these encounters? It is because I view life from a heavenly, eternal perspective. Bill Bright, the founder of Campus Crusade for Christ, once said, "If I am in a conversation with someone for five minutes or more, I believe it is a divine appointment for me to share the Gospel." Why would Bill Bright say something like that? Because he lived his life from an eternal perspective.

Did you know that one of the top reasons why Christians don't share the Gospel is because they view life from a temporal or temporary perspective rather than an eternal or heavenly perspective? Oliver Wendell Holmes Sr, a physician and poet, said, "Some people are so heavenly minded that they are no earthly good." I believe that the exact opposite is true of much of the church in America today. We are so earthly minded we are of no heavenly good. He was referring to the fact that some people are so wrapped up in church activities they have no impact on the world around them.

Sad to say, today, many Christians are so passionate about causes and issues in our world that they have forgotten the main issue, people's eternal destiny. We have become so focused on people's physical, emotional, mental, social, and safety needs that we have moved away from their spiritual needs. We want people to be healthy and happy. We have switched from the critical importance of "are people saved or are they lost?" to "are people blessed and happy in the here and now?" Don't get me wrong, Jesus cared about the health and welfare needs of people. He healed the sick; He delivered them from mental and emotional afflictions and even fed them. But Jesus' primary focus and purpose for coming was to seek and save those who were lost. Jesus said, "What if a man gains the whole world but loses his soul? What will a man give in exchange for his soul?" What if every earthly need a person has is met, but they spend eternity in hell separated from God?

The first-century church believed that Jesus was coming back at any time. They were driven by the mandate that the Gospel needed to be preached to every person on the planet. "Therefore, those who had been scattered went through *places* preaching the word" (Acts 8:4, NASB). Healings, miracles, signs, and wonders were used to draw their attention to the reality of Jesus' resurrection and salvation. Healings and miracles weren't the end goal but the doors through which they saw the reality of life beyond the here and now and their need for Jesus. Why did they have such a passion for preaching the Gospel, even at the risk of their lives? Because they had an eternal perspective on life. They were desperately concerned about people's eternal destiny.

I remember when I was first saved and realized that without receiving Jesus, people were destined to spend an eternity in hell, separated from the presence of God. I realized that most, if not all, of my friends and family were not going to spend eternity in heaven. I was desperate to make sure that wouldn't happen. Every opportunity I could, I would talk to them about Jesus and their need for Him. I'm sure I was obnoxious from their viewpoint. But praise the Lord; eventually, many of my friends and most of my family members became believers. Through the years, I have attended many funerals of people I knew were not believers in Jesus Christ. I would cringe when the officiating pastor or person would say, "They're in a better place now." No, they are not! Unless you consider eternity in torment, unending pain, suffering, and absolute terror a better place.

I have heard many Christians quote the saying, "Preach the Gospel at all times and if necessary, use words." The quote was attributed to Saint Francis of Assisi. In fact, there is no proof that he ever said it. Certainly, our life should line up with the teachings of Jesus, but no one is saved by seeing someone's good works. They are saved by one thing, hearing the Gospel! Good works, love, and living a holy life may cause people to ask about what makes us different, but it is believing in the Gospel that saves them. The Apostle Peter tells us that we are to be ready to give an answer to the hope people see in us (1 Peter 3:15).

The Apostle Paul says, "I am not ashamed of the gospel, for it is the power of God for salvation to everyone who believes, to the Jew first and also to the Greek" (Romans 1:16, NASB). He goes on to say,

> *How then are they to call on Him in whom they have not believed? How are they to believe in Him whom they have not heard? And how are*

they to hear without a preacher? But how are they to preach unless they are sent? Just as it is written: 'HOW BEAUTIFUL ARE THE FEET OF THOSE WHO BRING GOOD NEWS OF GOOD THINGS!'

However, they did not all heed the good news; for Isaiah says, 'LORD, WHO HAS BELIEVED OUR REPORT?' So faith comes from hearing, and hearing by the word of Christ.

Romans 10:14–17 (NASB)

When you live your life from an earthly, temporal perspective, life is all about what is happening or not happening in the present. We ask ourselves questions like, "Am I happy or sad?" "Am I rich or poor?" "Am I fulfilled or unfulfilled?" "Does everyone like me or hate me?" "Do I feel good or feel bad?" "Am I a success or a failure?" Questions like these only matter if we see our life as only being the sixty to eighty years we live on this planet. King Solomon was probably the wisest man ever to live (besides Jesus, of course). He wrote a book in the Bible called Ecclesiastes. The whole book was about his experiment of finding ultimate fulfillment through every possible thing you could do and experience in this life. He experimented with every pleasure, every accomplishment, the attaining of great riches and wealth, and anything else his mind could desire. After doing it all, he concluded that all was vanity (empty or waste) and chasing after the wind. Why? Because when you view your life from a temporal perspective, it comes up empty and futile. God designed us to live from an eternal perspective and not a temporal perspective.

When you shift your perspective from temporal to eternal, it changes everything in your life: how you see life, how you see yourself, how you see others, how you see your purpose and reason for living, how you see your choices and decisions whether good or bad, even how you see your difficulties, challenges, pains, and sufferings. All drastically change! Now you determine what is important in life based on eternity and not the short time you live in this world. When you live from an eternal perspective, what you do in relation to your time, your money, your relationships, your talents, and your gifts radically changes. Once you get the revelation that you are going to live forever and that death is not the end nor the worst thing that can happen to you, your motivations in life are completely changed.

The Apostle Paul viewed sufferings and difficulties from an eternal perspective. He called them light afflictions when viewed from an eternal perspective. He writes,

> *For our momentary, light affliction is producing for us an eternal weight of glory far beyond all comparison, while we look not at the things which are seen, but at the things which are not seen; for the things which are seen are temporal, but the things which are not seen are eternal.*
>
> **2 Corinthians 4:17–18 (NASB)**

Have you ever thought about the difference between your life span and eternity? James, the brother of Jesus and lead elder of the church in Jerusalem wrote, "It is even a vapor that appears for a little time and then vanishes away" (James 4:14). That is a puff of your hairspray, and it is gone. What you and I do during our short puff on this planet has eternal ramifications. Francis Chan illustrated our life compared to eternity in one of his messages, using a rope to represent eternity. Let's imagine the rope is one hundred feet long. No, a thousand feet long. No, a billion feet long. Now let's take a black marker and put a dot on the rope. That dot represents our total span of life. The Apostle Paul writes, "Redeeming the time, because the days are evil" (Ephesians 5:16, KJV). "Redeem the time" means "to make the most of your time." Make your time here on earth count the most for eternity.

When you live your life from an eternal perspective, acts of obedience come easy! Why? Because obeying the Lord is more important than the repercussions or consequences of your obedience. In 1 Samuel 15, King Saul, the first king of Israel, loses his future kingship. Why? Because his desire to be popular and respected by the people was more important to him than obeying God. In Genesis 25, Esau gave up his birthright to Jacob to gratify his hunger. Both men were focused on their earthly needs rather than eternal rewards. When you live from an eternal perspective, you will have courage and a willingness to sacrifice momentary gratification for the sake of the eternal benefits you will receive.

By faith Moses, when he had grown up, refused to be called the son of Pharaoh's daughter, choosing rather to endure ill-treatment with the people of God than to enjoy the temporary pleasures of sin, considering the reproach of Christ greater riches than the treasures of Egypt; for he was looking to the reward.

Hebrews 11:24–26 (NASB)

You see, Moses didn't care about Pharaoh's opinion or his earthly status and comfort. Moses cared about pleasing God and his eternal status and reward.

The Apostle Paul lived from the same perspective as Moses.

And now, behold, bound by the Spirit, I am on my way to Jerusalem, not knowing what will happen to me there, except that the Holy Spirit solemnly testifies to me in every city, saying that chains and afflictions await me. But I do not consider my life of any account as dear to myself, so that I may finish my course and the ministry which I received from the Lord Jesus, to testify solemnly of the gospel of God's grace.

Acts 20:22–24 (NASB)

Why don't you make the decision right now that you are going to live your life from an eternal perspective!

Chapter Sixteen

WHO IS MY NEIGHBOR?

A few years ago, a young couple moved in next door to our townhome. They seemed to be a nice young couple. Just one thing, they really liked their music! Now I had no problem with that at all until they wanted us to like their music as much as they did. I don't think they had any hearing issues, but they played their music so loud that it came through our adjoining wall from their townhome to ours. Their bass speakers were so powerful that they vibrated our furniture, and we could even feel them vibrating our bodies as well. I had not welcomed them to the neighborhood at this point. Now I had to go over to their front door and knock loud enough for them to hear it. The young husband came to the door, and I told him that I really didn't want to hear his music in my house. He gave me the look, "Nice meeting you too." I walked away thinking, *Way to go, Fred, that was a nice representation of Jesus' love. Not!* Anyhow, he turned the music down, and it was never a problem again. But I thought, *I just created a wall between us.*

Some months later, I pulled into my driveway, and there was a man standing in his driveway who had a brace on his knee. It turns out it was the young man's father. I asked him what happened to his leg, and he told me he had messed it up and was going to have it operated on the next week. I asked him if I could pray for him, and he said yes. I walked over to where he was and knelt in front of him and put my hands on his knee, and commanded healing into it in the name of Jesus. He thanked me for praying, and I went to my house. Some weeks later, I saw him in the driveway again without the brace. I asked him how his knee was doing, and he told me he didn't have to have the operation and his knee was fine.

Several months went by, and we were well into the 2020 pandemic. It was around Thanksgiving time, and I was sitting working at my computer in the middle of the afternoon, and my doorbell rang. When I answered the door, here was his son, my young neighbor, standing there. He asked me if he could borrow an egg because he was making some special dish that he traditionally did. I said, "Sure," and went and got two eggs and brought them out to him. Then he told me that the real reason that he came over was that he wanted me to pray for him. He said that he had been depressed and in bed for weeks because he had lost his job. Well, I encouraged him like a father would, telling him that it was all going to be okay and that we all go through difficult things. Then he said, "You don't understand; God made me come over here for you to pray for me." I told him that I have faith that when I pray for people for a job, they get one. Then I put my hand on his shoulder and prayed a simple prayer asking the Lord to get him a job.

A few weeks later, I saw him standing in his driveway and asked him how his job situation was. He apologized for not telling me sooner. He said that the very next day, after I prayed for him, he got two job offers from companies he hadn't even applied for. He took one of the jobs. He told me they were already paying him even before he officially started working for them. At Christmas, the doorbell rang again, and there stood my neighbor and his father holding gift baskets for us. The young neighbor said, "You are the only neighbors we are doing this for because we love you!" All this because of my one act of obedience of walking across to my neighbor's driveway and offering to pray for his knee.

This experience reminds me of another man named Ananias in the Book of Acts, chapter 9. I know I mentioned Ananias in an earlier chapter, but he is a good example of someone who almost reasoned his way out of a miracle encounter. He was sitting in his house minding his own business when he heard the voice of God telling him about a man named Saul, who was a Jewish Pharisee. The Lord told him that Saul was staying at a house on a street called "Straight" and was blind because of an encounter he had with Jesus speaking to him from heaven. The Lord told Ananias that He wanted him to go and pray for Saul to be healed and to tell him God's plan for his life. Ananias told the Lord that he had heard about Saul and that he was going around arresting and persecuting followers of Jesus. The Lord said to Ananias, "Go for he is a chosen vessel of Mine who will preach the Gospel to the Jews, to kings, and to the Gentiles." Ananias took the risk and went to find Saul and prayed for him to be healed from his blindness and to be filled with the Holy Spirit.

Most Christians know about Saul, who became the great Apostle, Paul. But very few know about the brave Ananias who was willing to risk his safety to go and pray for this persecutor of the church. And through his one act of obedience, Saul was launched into his divine destiny, which is impacting the world even to the present. Maybe there is a Saul in your neighborhood that the Lord has prepared for a disciple like you to visit and send them on their divine destiny. All it takes is for you to be willing and obedient when the Lord calls on you.

As to the question, "Who is my neighbor?" A lawyer was encountering Jesus, asking Him what he needed to do to inherit eternal life. Jesus asked him what the Law, speaking of the Old Testament, said about it. The lawyer answered, "You shall love the Lord your God with all your heart, with all your soul, with all your strength, and with all your mind, and love your neighbor as yourself." Jesus told him that was correct and to do that and he would live. But the lawyer, wanting to justify himself, said, "And who is my neighbor?"

Jesus told him the story of a Jewish man who was attacked and beaten up by robbers and was left for dead on the side of the road. Later a Jewish priest came by and saw the man and just walked by him as if he wasn't there. Then a Jewish Levite passed by and saw him as well but also acted like he wasn't even there and walked on by. A while later, a Samaritan man on a business trip came by, and when he saw the man, he felt compassion for him and went to him and bandaged up his wounds, pouring oil and wine on them. Then he picked him up and put him on his donkey and took him to a nearby inn and paid for his lodging until he recovered from his wounds. Then Jesus asked the lawyer, "Which of the three was the man's neighbor?" The lawyer answered, "The one who showed mercy on him." Jesus told the lawyer, "Go and do likewise."

"Who is my neighbor?" This is a good question for us as followers of Jesus today. Today in America, we Christians can get in our car in our garage, open our garage door, go do our tasks, drive back to our house, open the garage door, pull into our garage, close the garage door, and never come into contact with our neighbor. My brothers and sisters, there are people all around us who have been wounded and beat up by the devil. The opportunities for us to be their good Samaritan are endless. We just need to walk around with our spiritual eyes open and be willing to stop, get out of our little bubble world, and reach out to them with the love and compassion of Jesus!

A man asked Jesus what the greatest commandment was. Jesus' answer was, "To love God with all your heart, all your soul, all your mind, and all your strength. And the second is to love your neighbor as yourself." What does it mean "to love our neighbor as ourselves"? It means that we can no longer walk through our daily life and not care about the needs of our neighbors and especially the spiritual needs of our neighbors. Are they saved? Do they know about Jesus? Have they heard the Gospel? Do they know about His love for them? Are they going to spend eternity in heaven or hell? Have we taken the time to stop and hear their story? Have we prayed for the Lord to open a door for the Gospel in their lives?

Love is the bridge over which the Gospel travels. Theodore Roosevelt said, "Nobody cares how much you know until they know how much you care." We are living in an egocentric, narcissistic world where people only have themselves on their minds. Because of this, we have the opportunity to stand out like shining lights reaching out with a hand of hope.

I trust this chapter has opened your eyes to see the hurting neighbors all around you!

Chapter Seventeen

DOLLAR STORE ENCOUNTER

Another secret to seeing the Lord work through you is to live your life on mission. When a Christian decides they are called to be a missionary to a certain country or people group, they see themselves differently. They go believing that God has called them to preach the Gospel, make disciples and demonstrate the kingdom of God to people from a different culture. In other words, they understand their mission and purpose for getting out of bed every day. Every day, they devote their time, energy, and resources to reaching out to the lost and bringing them into the fellowship of believers.

The fact is that every born-again Christian is a missionary sent to a people in a foreign land. Jesus, in His prayer in John 17, prayed, "They are not of this world even as I am not of this world." Jesus went on in His prayer and prayed, "As you sent me into the world, I have also sent them into the world." Did you catch that? We are not of this world, and we have been sent into the world for the same purpose that Jesus was sent into the world, to seek and save those who are lost. When you live your life on mission, the Holy Spirit begins to orchestrate your life into what some call divine appointments. Below is an example of one of those divine appointments that my wife, Pam, experienced. In her own words:

"Sometimes when you least expect it, God moments show up. I am learning to trust that as we pray each day and present ourselves to God (Romans 12:1) that sometimes even our 'mistakes' can be a divine orchestration of His purpose.

"My elderly mother would use circle-a-word books to keep her mind active. I would usually get them at the Dollar Tree at a greatly reduced price. I bought quite a few to take to her. She lived about four hours away, and I forgot to bring them to her house. I apologized for the books when we left in the car to run some errands for her. In the process of running errands, we drove into a parking lot, and right there in front of us was a Dollar Tree. Wow, I realized all was not lost. We stopped. Mom wanted to wait in the car, but she shared she wanted one extra item besides the books I was getting for her. I went inside to look for the books and her additional item. I was quickly able to find the books and then asked the lady who was stocking the shelves where I would find the item my mom requested.

"The lady pointed down the aisle, and then she decided to stop stocking the shelf and lead me to another area around the corner of the aisle that had

a wider variety of items. I thanked her, and I went to stand in line to make the purchases, and I noticed the line was rather long. At times like this, I have learned rather than being frustrated, I start asking the Lord, 'Who do I need to talk to?' and 'Lord, are You setting up a divine appointment?' He encouraged me to go back to the lady who was so helpful, and she was now back stocking shelves. I thanked her again for her helpfulness and told her that she is God's treasure to me to go above and beyond to help me. I gave her one of our wristbands that says, 'I am God's Treasure,' and it glows in the dark.

"She looked stunned and then said, 'You know I didn't know how I was going to make it through this day; I just lost my mom!' (Wow, here I am looking for things for my mom, who was sitting outside in the car.) I felt so much compassion for her. I told her the Lord wanted her to know He saw her situation and wanted to assure her that He wanted to help her. I asked her, 'What is your name?' She said, 'Rose.' She started to cry and then began wailing. I could feel her pent-up emotions and pain. People were starting to look down the aisle, and I asked her if I could pray for her. She said yes. So, right there in the Dollar Tree store, I prayed for the peace and comfort of the Holy Spirit, and she began to calm down. I prayed for the awareness of God's love for her and the realization that God was reaching out to her to help her. All she had to do was to reach out to Him. She asked me if I was an angel. I said no, but God wanted her to know that in the midst of her pain and sorrow, Jesus was demonstrating to her that He really loved her. She asked if she could give me a hug. I said yes, and her tears pressed against my face. The reality of her hurt impacted me. She told me she felt so peaceful now!

"I left with so much joy, and I asked the Lord, 'How do you do that? How out of my 'mistake' and my prayer of 'Here I am, Lord, send me,' You arrange an answer to my prayer to meet Rose's need in a store that I have never been to before, in a city four hours away from where I live?' I realized what I thought was a 'mistake' was a rerouting of my schedule to touch the life of a hurting woman with God's love.

"It sounded like a story in the Bible when Jesus and the disciples were going across the sea of Galilee, probably not knowing they were going there for Jesus to set one severely demonized man free (Mark 5:1–20). The man had been terribly tormented for years, constantly crying out. He lived in the graveyard and cut himself with stones. No one was able to control or help him until Jesus and the disciples ended up on the shore where he was.

"While thinking about this experience, I communicated to the Lord, 'Thank you for letting me be a part of Rose's life and ministering your love to her.' I heard the Lord say, 'Thank you for listening and being my ambassador to minister my life and my love to Rose. I needed someone to be my hands and feet to respond to Rose's need.' Every so often, I pray for Rose as the Lord brings her to my mind. I know her life is on a journey to know the reality of God and Jesus as her Savior."

This is what living life on mission looks like. Maybe this is a new revelation for you, and you didn't realize that you are a missionary sent by the Lord Jesus Christ to the lost souls you will come in contact with. Now that you know, you can begin to pray like Pam, "Here I am, Lord, send me!" As you pray this prayer, get ready for the divine appointments that God has planned for you!

Chapter Eighteen

MY NAME IS INIGO MONTOYA

Set-Ups for Divine Appointments

In the late eighties, I was leading a mission trip team in Guatemala. We were building a new church building for a church near Antigua, a tourist city with lots of history. We checked into our hotel on a Saturday night and went to bed. The next morning, I woke up early, and a phrase from a movie called *The Princess Bride* was echoing over and over in my mind. "My name is Inigo Montoya; you killed my father, prepare to die!" It even had the accent the actor, Mandy Patinkin, used playing Inigo. Dan, our church worship leader, was asleep in the bed next to mine. I jumped on top of him and started shaking him, yelling, "My name is Inigo Montoya; you killed my father, prepare to die!" Dan woke up and looked at me and said, "What's wrong with you?" I said, "I don't know; this phrase keeps going through my mind over and over."

A little later, I needed to go to the hotel lobby to see

about getting a room for us to have a church service with the team. To get there, I had to walk through the hotel restaurant. As I walked through, I noticed out of the corner of my eye that there was one person sitting in the restaurant. As I looked over at him, he looked like one of the actors from the movie. It was Vizzini, the Sicilian criminal, bully, and mastermind employed by Prince Humperdinck to kidnap Princess Buttercup. He was the one who always used the phrase, "That's inconceivable!" I walked over and asked him if it was him, and he said, "Yes." I told him how much my daughters loved the movie. I asked him what his name was, and he said, "Wally Shawn." He kind of gave me the "I am annoyed" look, implying, "Go away, I don't really want to talk to anyone." So, I went on to the lobby. On my way back to my room, I thought, *Wow, what a coincidence!* That I would meet one of the actors from the movie after having that phrase go through my mind over and over. Then, it was like the Holy Spirit was knocking on my head saying, "Hello, Fred, this was not a coincidence!" I told Dan what had happened, and he was surprised as well.

The next morning, we had breakfast early in the restaurant before we went out to work on the church. Guess who walks up to the table. That's right; it was Wally. He said, "Would you mind if I had breakfast with you?" I said, "Yes, join us." He asked, "What are you guys doing here?" I told him that we were Christians from a church near Kansas City and that we were building a new church building for an indigenous church here. He was telling us about himself and that he was from a Jewish family in New York City. I asked him what he was doing here. After looking around the room to see if anyone was listening, he said he was writing a political play about America. He believed America was a bad country. Why? Because, in his opinion, we had hurt countries like El Salvador by supporting their military financially. As he was talking, one of my team members, Paul, who was a former motorcycle gang biker before he gave his life to Jesus, walked up to our table to ask me some questions about today's activities. Paul had tattoos all over his arms, including a Nazi swastika. When Wally saw that, he said, "What kind of church are you?" I told him about Paul's testimony and how Jesus had completely changed his life. At the end of the breakfast, Wally told us that he and his girlfriend were leaving to go to another hotel in Guatemala City, and we wouldn't see him again.

We came back to the hotel later that night after a full day of working on the new church building. We were tired and had to walk through the restaurant on our way to our rooms. As we walked through, there was Wally waiting for us. He asked me to come and meet his Jewish girlfriend. Just as we got to their table, a waiter came up to Wally and told him that he had a call from someone from New York and to take it in the hotel lobby. He left me there with his girlfriend, who proceeded to tell me how Wally had told her all about me and that they wanted to have dinner with me and anyone I would like to bring along this week. Evidently, they had decided to stay at the hotel for a few more days. It was Monday, so I set it for Wednesday night; that way, it gave me and our team time to pray for the meeting with them.

Wednesday night, I took Dan with me, and we met them at a small Italian restaurant owned by a Sicilian man who was hiding out from the mafia here in Guatemala. I had met him earlier that week, and when he found out that my grandparents were from Sicily, he told me his situation. But that is a story for another time. As soon as we sat down with Wally and his girlfriend, Deborah Eisenberg, Wally pulled out a notepad and looked at me, and said, "Alright, tell me your story!" So I shared my testimony with them. As I talked, his girlfriend, Deborah, had tears streaming down her face. When I finished, he turned to Dan and said, "Now tell me your story!" He literally took notes while we shared. While I was talking, the owner of the restaurant came over to our table and said, "Do you realize that everyone is listening to you?" I thought, *I must have been talking pretty loudly.* The owner said, "It is because of him," pointing to Wally; "we all recognize him." It looks like we got to give our testimonies to everyone in the restaurant. After dinner, we were standing outside the restaurant with them, and I asked them if they would like to receive Jesus' salvation. Wally answered for them both and told us they weren't ready to do that yet. So I asked if we could lay hands on them and pray for them, and they said, "Yes." So, Dan and I prayed for them. The next day they left for Guatemala City. I ran into them one more time at a hotel there and took a picture together with them.

So, let's process this story. When we are willing to be used by the Lord to be a witness for Him, He arranges things in our lives that are beyond the realm of coincidence. I watch a movie that has one line in it repeated over and over throughout the movie. I travel to Guatemala on a specific day and wake up with that line going through my mind repeatedly. I run into a main actor from the movie, who is a Jew. He wants to have dinner with me to hear my testimony. What are the odds of all this coming together? The Lord wants to reach lost people with the message of the Gospel that He will arrange your whole life and decisions to set up a divine appointment for you and me to step into.

WALLY SHAWN, FRED KROPP, AND WALLY'S GIRLFRIEND

Divine appointments: what are they, and how do we see an increase in them in our lives?

What is a "divine appointment"?

A divine appointment is when the person with the power or solution meets the person with the need. A divine appointment is an opportunity orchestrated by the Holy Spirit for the Gospel of the kingdom to be shared with a lost soul. "And at the same time pray for us also, that God may open a door to us for the Word (the Gospel), to proclaim the mystery concerning Christ (the Messiah) on account of which I am in prison" (Colossians 4:3, AMPC).

What are some of the signs that may indicate the Lord is setting up a divine appointment for you?

1. You experience a change or interruption in your schedule:

One time I was traveling with one of my associates in New Haven, Connecticut, when our flight out of New Haven was canceled. People started getting very angry at the agent working the airline counter. One lady stood out who seemed very upset. I walked up to her and asked her why she was so upset. She told me that because of the cancellation, she was going to miss a very important event she had to be at. I said to her, "Let me solve your problem." I went up to the counter and told the agent that she was doing a great job! I asked her if there were any other alternatives. The agent said that there were flights available that would get the lady and us where we wanted to go on time at the airport in

Hartford, which was thirty-nine miles away. I told the agent to rebook us there, then got a cab for the lady and us to take us to Hartford. During the ride there, we had the opportunity to tell her all about Jesus and pray with her to know Him.

2. You feel a sudden urge that you need to be at a certain place right now:

One day I was sitting at home, and suddenly, I felt the need to go to our local Walmart to get something I didn't really need to get right then. I could get it anytime; why right now? I went to Walmart and got my item. On the way out, while walking to my car, I noticed a young man walking very slowly, looking like he was in pain. I started to walk past him but then thought I should go and ask him what was wrong. When I approached him, he looked at me like I was a weirdo or something. He said that he had a serious back problem. I told him that I understood what that was like as I have had back problems in the past. I told him that I was a Christian and that I believed Jesus healed people. I asked if I could pray for him, and he said yes. I laid my hand on his shoulder and prayed for his back. After I did, he wanted to know what church I went to and where it was. I told him about our church and that it was filled with people just like him. I hadn't seen him there yet, but as I drove out of the parking lot, I knew why I felt the urge to go to Walmart.

3. You experience a feeling of compassion toward someone or some group of people:

Many of the miracles that Jesus did were preceded by the phrase, "And Jesus, being moved with compassion." One of the main ways the Holy Spirit leads us into divine appointments is through feelings of compassion. Romans 5:5 says that the love of God has been poured out in our hearts through the Holy Spirit. When you start to have a feeling of compassion or mercy toward someone, that can very well be an indicator of a divine appointment. When you are going through your daily life, ask the Lord to make you more aware of His love toward the people you encounter, and you will find yourself being moved by His compassion.

4. A specific person or thought comes to your mind:

Another sign of a possible divine appointment being set up to happen is when a person or a thought comes to your mind. "You should give them a call; you should go over and talk with them." It is just a subtle prompting of the Holy Spirit that can lead to a miracle happening in someone else's life. In the Gospel of John, chapter 4, Jesus and the disciples are headed back to Galilee from Judea. Jesus told the disciples that He had to go through Samaria, which was out of their way. It was there that Jesus met a Samaritan woman and revealed Himself to her as the Jewish Messiah. His encounter with her impacted her life so powerfully that she went and told everyone in town about it. This led to nearly the whole community believing in Jesus. What led Jesus to determine that He needed to go through Samaria? It very well could have been a thought or an impression that He needed to go there. I have to ask myself the question, "Am I that sensitive and willing to be used by God that He could send me to a potential person who He will use to change the world for Jesus?"

Here are some simple bullet points that will open up more divine appointments in your life:

- let the Lord know you are available to be used by Him;

- ask Him to open doors of opportunity to share the Gospel;

- be willing to take a risk;

- be daily filled with the Word of God and the Holy Spirit; and

- step out by faith into grace.

Chapter Nineteen

GIVE ME THE FACTS

What I am about to explain to you has the power to radically transform your life. Many years ago, Bill Bright, the founder of Campus Crusade for Christ, created a booklet called *The Four Spiritual Laws*. In the book, there was a picture of a train with three cars, an engine, a coal car, and a caboose. One word was written on each car. On the engine was the word "Fact." On the coal car was the word "Faith." And on the caboose was the word "Feeling." It showed that the Christian life should not be based on feelings, circumstances, or experiences but on facts that are activated by faith. If you and I are going to live the supernatural Christian life, we must live it by faith that is based on facts from God's Word. For definition purposes for this chapter, I am defining a "fact" as an absolute, unchangeable truth found in the Bible.

One of the things that hinder many Christians from doing acts of obedience is that they live their lives based on feelings, experiences, and circumstances. "Do I feel like stepping out and talking to some stranger?" "The last time I prayed for someone to be healed, nothing happened!" "If God makes the opportunity obvious, then I will do it." "I really don't see myself qualified to minister to someone else. In fact, I need someone to minister to me." "I don't believe that I can be bold!" Statements, thoughts, and reasonings like these are based on the lies and fears the enemy wants us to believe, not the facts of God's Word.

Let me give you an example of an unchangeable fact. My name is Fred Kropp; that is a fact based on historical evidence. Someone may call me Joe Smith, but that doesn't change the fact that I am Fred Kropp. I might have days where I get up and don't feel like I am Fred Kropp, but that doesn't change the fact that I am. A friend that hasn't seen me for years may not recognize me when they see me, but that still doesn't change the fact that I am Fred Kropp. What does all this mean? It means that nothing can change the fact of who I am! Now let's apply this to our Christian life.

There are facts in the Bible that do not change no matter what we think, believe, feel, or what circumstances contrary to them show us. Let's establish some of those facts. Jesus, God's only begotten Son, came to earth, became a man, lived a perfect life, died on a cross, was buried, rose from the dead on the third day, and now is seated at the right hand of God in heaven waiting for His enemies to become a footstool under His feet. Nothing you or I think, believe, feel, or observe with our five senses can ever change that fact. There are other Bible facts about you and me that are also true and unchangeable. Let's look at some of those facts.

Here are twenty-one facts that happened when you decided to believe in Jesus Christ:

1. You died with Jesus on the cross (Galatians 2:20);

2. You were buried with Jesus in His death (Romans 6:3–4);

3. You rose with Jesus into resurrection life (Romans 6:5);

4. You died to your sinful nature and were made alive to God (Romans 6:11);

5. You were transferred out of Satan's kingdom into the kingdom of God's Son (Colossians 1:13);

6. You became a new creation in Christ (a new species of people) (2 Corinthians 5:17);

7. The old person you used to be passed away (1 Corinthians 5:17);

8. Jesus Christ has come to live inside of you (Colossians 1:27);

9. You became the temple of the Holy Spirit (1Corinthians 6:19);

10. You became the righteousness of God in Christ (2 Corinthians 5:21);

11. You became a joint heir with Christ (Romans 8:17);

12. You became a member of God's family (Ephesians 2:19);

13. You gained right standing with God, the Father (Romans 5:1);

14. You have been given authority over sin, the world, the devil and his demons (Luke 10:19);

15. You are seated with Christ in heavenly places (Ephesians 2:6);

16. You are under the blessing of Abraham (Galatians 3:13–14);

17. You are set free from the curse of the Law (Galatians 3:13);

18. You are no longer under the judgment of God (John 5:24);

19. You have a new purpose and destiny (Ephesians 2:10);

20. You have access to God's throne of grace (Ephesians 3:11–12; Hebrews 4:16); and

21. You have eternal and abundant life (John 10:10).

To walk in and experience these facts, we must set our focus on them and refuse to look at things in our lives that are contrary to or in opposition to them. The Apostle Paul calls it "walking by faith and not by sight and setting our minds on things above, not on things on the earth" (2 Corinthians 5:7; Colossians 3:2). We now have all these things "in Christ." When you and I were baptized, the Apostle Paul tells us in Galatians 3:27 that we were baptized into Christ and have put on Christ. So, another fact is that we are in Christ, and because we are in Him, all the promises of God are yes and amen, to the glory of God, through us (1 Corinthians 1:20). So, why are we not experiencing them? Because we keep shifting our attention to what we see, feel and think instead of fixing our focus on the facts of God's promises in Christ. Rest assured that the enemy of our souls is doing everything he can to get us to focus on our circumstances, feelings, thoughts, and opinions rather than the facts of God's Word. In other words, he wants to get us out of Christ and the truth of who we are in Him. If he can rob us of our true identity, then he can keep us from doing acts of obedience. The more we focus on the facts of our true identity, the more we will make an eternal difference in the world around us.

The more I focus on the facts of my identity in Christ, the more I live out my life knowing why I am here on this planet. I am here for the same reason Jesus was, to seek and save those who are lost, to proclaim the Gospel of the kingdom, to go about doing good and healing those who are oppressed by the devil. When I teach my identity series, I start with the statement, "If you know who you are, then you know why you are here. If you know why you are here, then you know what to do, and if you know what to do, then you know where to go." Knowing the facts takes away the mystery of life. You are an ambassador for Christ, a representative of His kingdom, wherever you go and whatever you do. You are here to do the works of Jesus! Don't allow the enemy to steal the facts from you! Become an expert in knowing and focusing on the facts and not on your feelings, symptoms, or circumstances.

Let me give you an example. My wife, Pam, and I have tithed faithfully during our whole fifty-plus years of marriage. Even though we tithed, we didn't experience the windows of heaven opening over our lives like we saw in other believers' lives until twenty years ago. Just in case you are thinking that we were tithing to get money, no, we were tithing out of obedience to the Word of God. But the reality was we were just barely making it financially every month. In my Bible reading one day, I was reading in Galatians that Jesus became a curse for us that we might be under the blessing of Abraham. I had read that passage hundreds of times, but this time, it jumped off the page at me. I saw the fact that I was under the blessing of Abraham. I went to look at how blessed Abraham was and found in Genesis 24 that he was blessed in every area of his life. I began to say and pray every day, "I am under the blessing of Abraham!" If you were to run into me and ask how I was doing, I would say, "I'm under the blessing of Abraham!" I did this for a whole year without seeing any change in our financial situation. Then suddenly, almost a year later to the day I started saying it, the windows of heaven opened over our lives and have stayed open ever since.

What happened? Without understanding what I was doing, I was focusing on the fact and not on what I was experiencing. As we did this, faith came, and the fact became a reality in our lives. The Book of Hebrews says that through faith and patience, we inherit the promises.

What if we focus on other Bible facts that we don't see active in our lives? Like the works that Jesus did, I can do! Or, I have received power to be a bold witness for Jesus! As we refuse to believe anything other than these biblical facts, and we begin to say them and pray them over our lives every day, then, over time, those facts will become our new reality.

What are some biblical facts that are not active in your life? Pick one and start confessing out loud Scriptures that declare them in your life!

Chapter Twenty
ACCIDENTAL MIRACLES

Sometimes God does miracles that have very little to do with your faith but with your getting out on a limb called risk. During the early nineties, our church was participating in feeding the homeless on the streets of Kansas City. I had a minister friend who had a building downtown, who used it to feed and care for the homeless. Every Friday night, a church would volunteer to cook and bring in all the food to feed them. They would also provide Christian entertainment with a presentation of the Gospel. Our time was every third Friday of the month. We had done this several times and always came up with some creative way to present the Gospel. Sometimes it was our worship team, a soloist, or a skit. It always went over well! One Friday night, we were there and were preparing to serve the dinner when I realized we had forgotten to prepare any entertainment following the meal.

I was searching in my mind for an idea, and something crazy just popped into my head. So, just before we started eating, I asked the crowd there if anyone had seen a miracle. They all shook their head no. Without thinking, I blurted out, "Right after the dinner tonight, God is going to do a miracle!"

I walked back into the kitchen and thought, *What did I just say? I can't make a miracle happen. Why did I tell them that?* I spent the rest of the meal in the kitchen thinking, *When they finish eating, they're probably just going to jet out back onto the streets.* I waited as long as I could to give them plenty of time to leave. When I finally opened the kitchen door to look, there they all were, waiting for me to come out and work a miracle. Not one single person had left. I walked out and said, "Is everyone ready to see a miracle?" They were on the edge of their seats. By the look on their faces, I better produce a miracle, or my physical safety might be in jeopardy. I tried to think of some low-level miracle that wouldn't be so obvious as to whether it happened or not. I said, "Does anyone have a leg problem?"

A guy sitting near me said, "I do!" I went over and asked which leg, and he said, "Both!" I thought, *Okay, he probably has some pain in his legs, so this might be a safe one to try.* I asked further, "What seems to be the problem?" He said, "I've got this leg disease, and I can hardly walk." Then he proceeded to roll up his pants, and I was looking at the sickest-looking legs I had ever seen. They had scales and rotting areas of flesh on them. I thought, *Lord! There's no way I am laying hands on this!* By this time, everyone was out of their seats, crowded around me, looking over one another's shoulders and even standing on chairs to get a good view of the miracle. I spoke out loudly, "I command these legs to be healed in the name of Jesus!" I looked at his legs, and nothing changed. I said it again; still nothing. I thought, *This is not good.* Then, I told him to stand up and try his legs. He stood up and gently put pressure on one and then the other. Then he stepped a little harder and yelled out, "Hey! Hey! My legs are better!" Then he began to jump up and down, yelling the same thing even louder. With that, the whole crowd went crazy, and others started saying, "Heal me! Heal me!" I thought, *Thank You, Jesus!* That was a close one!

Obviously, this miracle had very little to do with my faith, wisdom, or courage. So, what was happening here? I don't know how much the Lord cares about protecting my reputation, but He is totally committed to protecting His. Moses writes in Numbers 23:19, "God *is* not a man, that He should lie, nor a son of man, that He should repent. Has He said, and will He not do? Or has He spoken, and will He not make it good?" In other words, if God says He will do something, He does it! Another passage says that God watches over His word to perform it. In the Gospel of Mark 16:20, it says that as the disciples went everywhere preaching, the Lord confirmed His word with signs following. God delights in performing His word. Acts 10:38 tells us that Jesus went about doing good and healing all who were oppressed by the devil, for God was with Him. Remember, God wants to touch people more than they want to be touched.

Another element in this accidental miracle was "the risk factor"! The circumstances forced me to take a risk I probably wouldn't have chosen to take. For us to see more of the miracles we see Christians working in the New Testament, we must take more risks. We must remove the negative "buts and what ifs" out of our vocabulary. "But what if I am not hearing the Lord correctly?" "But what if I pray for them and nothing happens?" "But what if I share Jesus with them, and they tell me to go away?" We replace the negative "buts and what ifs" with positive "buts and what-ifs." "But what if I am hearing from the Lord?" "But what if they do get healed?" "But what if they accept the Gospel and are saved?"

Think about Peter and John standing in front of the man crippled from birth at the beautiful gate of the temple and Peter thinking, *What if I grab this guy's hand and lift him up, and he just falls over on his face? Won't that be a great witness for Jesus!* Instead, Peter's willingness to take the risk resulted in crowds of people, including the religious leaders of Jerusalem, hearing the Gospel. Even the high priest got to hear about Jesus because of this miracle. What have we got to lose? (I'm speaking to myself now.) A moment of embarrassment. A prayer that didn't get answered instantly. A rejection of the Gospel. What have we got to win? An opportunity to plant the seed of the Gospel in the heart of someone who very well may respond to it in the future. A healing that could cause them to tell others about Jesus and their family coming to Christ! I have prayed for many people who didn't get healed on the spot. Almost all of them thanked me for praying for them. Why? Because they appreciated the fact that I cared about them.

God's Son, Jesus Christ, came to earth and took the risk of suffering and dying on the cross, with no guarantee that anyone would ever believe in Him and receive free salvation through His grace. If He was willing to pay such a high price and take such a risk for us, how could we not take the little risks that can make the difference between heaven and hell for those we meet? People, whether they are Christians or not, take risks all the time for rewards and benefits that hold no comparison to eternal life. Our risks are for the highest purpose, a soul going from death to life for all eternity.

What are some areas of risk that the Lord wants you to step out on?

Chapter Twenty-One

YOU ARE QUALIFIED!

I had been pastoring a small floundering church for a few years with little success when I got a phone call from the secretary of a pastor of a very successful growing church in a nearby town. She said that the pastor wanted to meet with me at his office that afternoon. When I got there, the secretary informed me that he was going to be a few minutes late and took me into his office to wait for him. As I sat there, I couldn't help but notice all the plaques and certificates of multiple degrees he had earned. Some of the plaques said, "I'm number one!" or indicated one of the many awards he had received over the years. The longer I sat there, the more intimidated I felt because I didn't have any of those plaques on the walls of my office. I thought, *What am I doing in the ministry? I am so unqualified to be doing what I am doing!*

When the pastor finally came in, he thanked me for taking the time to come and meet with him. Then, to my shock, he said, "The reason I asked you to come is that

I need your advice and input on a situation I am dealing with." I thought, *You have all the plaques and awards, and you want my advice?* We spent an hour together, and I was able to help him with his situation. He thanked me and let me know how much he appreciated me.

During my ten-mile drive back to my office, all I could think about was all those degrees and awards he had. I continued to struggle with how unqualified I was to be pastoring a church. As I kept thinking about it, the Lord brought Colossians 1:12 to my mind, "Giving thanks to the Father who has qualified us to be partakers of the inheritance of the saints in the light," and said to me, "I have qualified you!" He was saying that He was the One who chose me, qualified me, and appointed me to do what I was doing and that I was to stop seeing myself as unqualified. Another scripture that came to my mind was in the Gospel of John 15:16, "You did not choose Me, but I chose you and appointed you that you should go and bear fruit, and *that* your fruit should remain, that whatever you ask of the Father in My name He may give you."

Maybe as you have read my stories of being used by the Lord to touch others' lives, you might think the way I did. You don't feel qualified or capable to be used by God in acts of obedience. But I believe that the Lord is saying to you, "I have qualified you! I have chosen you, and I have appointed you to bear fruit for My kingdom." When the Apostle Paul was faced with challenges and difficulties that were overwhelming to him, he said, "I can do all things through Christ who strengthens me."

When the Apostle John wrote about facing the spirit of the antichrist, he reminded us that He who is in us (speaking of the Holy Spirit) is greater than he (speaking of the devil) who is in the world. The Apostle Paul reminded the Christians in Corinth that they had the treasure of the Holy Spirit dwelling in their bodies so that the greatness of the power they functioned from came from God rather than their own abilities.

Allow me to encourage you today! You have the same power that raised Jesus from the dead dwelling in your body! You are qualified! You are well able! You are more than a conqueror in Christ! You are the miracle that is waiting to happen for someone today! Don't waste another minute thinking you can't do it! Remember that God chooses ordinary, messed-up people like you and me to do great things for His kingdom! You are God's instrument on the earth! You are the hands and feet of Jesus! There is a world full of hurting, lost people waiting to encounter you! You carry the answer they are looking for even if they don't know what they are looking for.

I was at the mall with another Christian brother, and we saw a young man sitting on the floor outside of a gymnastics school for little girls. You could see all the girls through the large glass windows. When we approached him, he jumped up and said, "I am not a pervert! I am waiting for my daughter, who is in the class!" We assured him that we were not there to judge him or think anything evil of him. We started to talk to him about what Jesus had done in our lives when a woman walked up and stood right next to me while I was talking. It was his wife. She listened intently as I shared. While I was sharing, he walked away from us, and she said that he didn't like hearing about religious stuff. Then she told us that they had just moved here to California for him to take a new job and also to get him away from a drug addiction culture he was caught in. Soon, he wandered back into the conversation, and I told them that they were great parents and that I was excited about their decision to move here. Then I asked him what his name was, and he said, "Adam." Without even thinking, I turned to his wife and said, "And you are Eve." She was startled and said, "How did you know?" I didn't; I was just making a joke. I asked them if my friend and I could pray for them, and they said yes. We prayed for their marriage and family and the new job. When we finished praying, I said, "Look at this, you came all the way here to California to have a new beginning in life." To which Eve said, "No, we came all the way to California to have this encounter with you!"

My friends, there are Adams and Eves that the Lord is going to bring into your life from near and far for them to hear the Gospel and encounter the love of God through you! You can do it! Come on! Say it out loud, "I can do all things through Christ who strengthens me" (Philippians 4:13).

Chapter Twenty-Two

IF YOU ARE WILLING AND OBEDIENT

Early in my Christian life, I heard a message by a man of God who the Lord used powerfully to reach hundreds of young people for Christ and disciple them. The message was titled, "Two keys to being used by God." The message was from the Book of Isaiah, chapter 1, verse nineteen: "If you are willing and obedient, you shall eat the good of the land." The message had a huge impact on my life. The two keys were our willingness to be used by the Lord and our obedience when He asks us to do something. Sounds simple right? I wanted to live this way but soon found that it was more challenging than I thought.

There have been times in my walk with Jesus where I struggled with being willing and obedient and have come up short. I would like to say that I have always been willing and obedient, but that has not always been the case. I have found that when I say, "No, I just can't do that," life becomes very difficult.

Many years back, I felt that I was called to full-time ministry, but it just wasn't working out. I was a ministerial student at a certain denomination's college studying for the ministry. Then the leaders of the denomination put out a statement that if you spoke in tongues, you were to leave the denomination. That created a problem for me because I did speak in tongues. I dropped out, giving up on my desire to be a full-time minister. At that time, I owned a business to support us while I was going through college. My business evolved into home building and commercial real estate. I concluded that the Lord wanted me to be in business instead of ministry. I believed I would make a lot of money for God's kingdom to support missionaries. The business was doing well, and I designed and built my family a house in a nice neighborhood, bought a new car, and focused on my success. At the same time, Pam and I were part of a team of Christians that ran a Christian halfway house that took hurting, messed up people off the streets. We took them through deliverance and discipled them.

One day I heard the Lord say to me, "Sell everything you own and follow Me." I thought that it was just a test to see if I was willing to do it, not that He literally wanted me to do it. At this time, I had a wife, two kids, a new car, nice suits, and a business that was poised to make big money. I even went to my church leaders and told them what I believed the Lord had said to me. They confirmed what I wanted to hear: that the Lord just wanted me to be willing to do it, not to actually do it. Then the bottom dropped out! We had a major recession hit the nation, which had a devastating impact on the building industry. My business went into a nosedive, but I kept working, believing that it was a test of my faith. I believed that a huge financial breakthrough was coming, so I kept right on running the business believing the turnaround was coming at any moment. During this time, our debts were piling up as we borrowed money from every source we could to keep ourselves afloat.

This went on for two years with a strange thing that repeatedly happened that kept my hopes up. Because I was a commercial real estate agent, I would put together a real estate agreement between a buyer and a seller that would guarantee me a huge commission. The commission was so big it would get us out of debt, but every time we would get to the closing table to finalize the deal, either the seller or buyer or both would back out of the deal. I couldn't believe it! What was happening? This happened over and over again, but I still believed that breakthrough was coming. Toward the end of the two years, everything we owned was going to be repossessed, our house, our car, our kids (just kidding). We had times when we literally had no food in the cupboards, and I was embarrassed to ask the church for help. Yet we never went without food. There were times when we would open the front door to find a bag of groceries on the porch. I found myself falling into a deep depression.

On top of this, during the two years, I only heard the

Lord speak to me a few times. I had been used to hearing His voice regularly. On one occasion, I was standing in the middle of my living room holding my Bible up, yelling at God, "Philippians 4:19 says that You will supply all my needs according to Your riches in glory in Christ Jesus! Do You believe this?" He decided to answer me. He said, "What if I never do anything for you again? Will you still follow Me?" I said, "Yes!" Another time, I was sitting in my car on the side of a nearby lake, deeply depressed, and I said to the Lord, "Your Word says that You won't tempt me beyond that which I can stand, and I can't stand anymore!" He chose to speak to me once again. He said, "You haven't hit the bottom yet!" I responded, "Then get me there right now!" A short time later, I was walking into my real estate office when I heard the Lord say to me, "If you keep going this direction, I will have to break both of your legs." I don't believe that the Lord breaks people's legs. It was just my interpretation of what I believed He was saying to me. I remembered where the Lord sought to kill Moses because he hadn't circumcised his sons. This really scared me. He was making it clear I was going in the wrong direction.

I went home and stayed in our guest room for two weeks, fasting and praying, saying, "What do You want?" During the second week, I got a call from a friend of mine who was pastoring a church in a small town south of Kansas City, Missouri. He asked what I was doing, and I told him, "Nothing." He said, "I'm going to plant another church in Kansas City, and I want you to come and pastor this church." I had visited his church some time back, and it wasn't one that I would want to pastor because it was in a little country town in a 118-year-old building. I told him I would pray for the person it would be but that it wasn't me. He said, "Well, you pray about it." I prayed in my room for a few more days and began to think, *It might be me.*

A few weeks later, the church sent us the money for Pam and me to travel to Missouri for ten days to see if this was the Lord. During the ten days, the Lord gave us multiple confirmations that we were to become the pastors there. We went home and packed up a trailer full of our few belongings and moved there. Another interesting thing is that while we were visiting the church for ten days, someone broke into our home in Idaho and stole several of our major appliances. This worked out in our favor, as the home insurance gave us enough money to be able to afford the move to Missouri. Just four months after we moved, our house in Idaho sold during a very bad market, and we were able to pay off all our debts. Even though I wasn't willing to sell everything and follow the Lord when He spoke to me, it ended up happening anyway. Sometimes when we are not willing, the Lord allows circumstances in our lives to humble us and make us willing and obedient. Maybe that's what the Apostle Paul meant when he wrote, "And we know that all things work together for good to those who love God, to those who are the called according to *His* purpose" (Romans 8:28). This wasn't the way I thought I would end up in the ministry, but the Lord had a plan very different from mine.

In a few short weeks, I went from being a broke real estate agent to being the pastor of a church. I have now been in full-time ministry for over forty years. I have pastored in three different churches in three different states. For a period of five years, I did one hundred and forty-five seminars in churches all over the USA. I have traveled and ministered in forty-one nations. I haven't always been as obedient as I should, but the Lord, in His lovingkindness and mercy, still allowed me to work for Him. In Romans 8:31, Paul writes, "If God *is* for us, who *can be* against us?" God has a plan for our lives that is far better than we could ever dream of. The key to walking in His plan is for us to be willing and obedient!

Jesus tells the story of a young, wealthy man who comes to Him and asks what he must do to inherit eternal life. Jesus told him to keep the commandments. The young man asked, "Which ones?" Jesus mentioned a few of them, and the young man told Jesus he had kept all of them since his youth. Jesus then told him that there was one more thing he needed to do, sell everything he owned, give the money to the poor and come and follow Him. The young man went away sad because he owned a lot of property and was very rich. The young man missed out on the greatest opportunity anyone can have, to be a disciple of Jesus and walk in the eternal destiny that was designed for him. Why? Because he was not willing and obedient.

Maybe you find yourself in the place where I was,

CHAPTER 22: IF YOU ARE WILLING AND OBEDIENT

knowing that the Lord has asked you to do something that you just don't believe you can do or are unwilling to give up something to obey Him. Don't be like the rich young man and miss your destiny or have to go through painful lessons like I did to get you there. Ask the Lord to help you to be willing and obedient and trust that His plan is far better than anything He asks you to give up. Jeremiah 29:11 says, "For I know the thoughts that I think toward you, says the LORD, thoughts of peace and not of evil, to give you a future and a hope." If you are reading this book, rest assured that I am praying for you to experience and walk in God's full plan for your life! He designed you to accomplish amazing things in your time here on this planet and has wonderful rewards awaiting you when you enter eternity. Don't miss out on them!

EPILOGUE

I hope that I have awakened the reader to the reality that the Lord wants to work through them to touch the lives of those they encounter with the Gospel of the kingdom! No doubt we are moving into the days that Jesus spoke about in Matthew 24. His disciples asked Him what the signs of the end times would be. He told them there would be wars and rumors of war, rampant diseases, earthquakes, and false prophets. But the last sign He mentioned was that the Gospel of the kingdom would be preached in all the world, and then the end would come. The Gospel of the kingdom is activated through our lives by simple acts of obedience! It is time for you and me, the body of Christ, to say, "Here I am, Lord, send me!"

I know that some of the experiences I have shared in this book may be out of the comfort zone of some. But I encourage you to start where you are and allow the Lord to increase your boldness as you go. Maybe it will be texting someone or buying someone's coffee as the Holy Spirit prompts you. There is a kingdom principle that says if we are faithful in a little thing, the Lord will give us greater things. Jesus said, "Greater love has no one than this, to lay down one's life for his friends." It simply means laying down what you want to do, your feelings, your fears, your apathy, and your time to help someone else encounter Jesus!

REFERENCES

Bright, Bill. *Have You Heard the Four Spiritual Laws?* Campus Crusade for Christ, 1952.

Merriam-Webster Online Dictionary. https://www.merriam-webster.com/

YourDictionary Online. https://www.yourdictionary.com/

ABOUT THE AUTHOR

Fred and his wife, Pam, have been married for over fifty years. They have four daughters and five grandchildren. Fred has been a pastor and a seminar instructor and has ministered in forty-one countries. His passion is to encourage and equip the next generation to know their identity in Christ and how to demonstrate God's kingdom through their everyday lives. He and Pam are the founders of As You Go Ministries, a ministry dedicated to activating Christians in sharing the Gospel. Fred and Pam serve out of The Healing Rooms Apostolic Center in Santa Maria, California, and they are a part of the teaching team at The Bridge Church Central Coast in Santa Maria. Fred has a biweekly Facebook and YouTube teaching broadcast.

https://www.facebook.com/fred.kropp

https://www.youtube.com/channel/ UCcL0vI4DL3x2_3_6wOY0MBw

You can contact them by email:
fkropp1948@gmail.com

Website: **fredkropp.com**

CPSIA information can be obtained
at www.ICGtesting.com
Printed in the USA
BVHW090007290622
640818BV00017B/1185